The

Satisfied

WORKBOOK

WORKBOOK

A SPIRITUAL GUIDE TO
Recovery and Food Freedom

DR. RHONA EPSTEIN, PSY.D

DEXTERITY
NASHVILLE

Dexterity, LLC
604 Magnolia Lane
Nashville, TN 37211

Printed in the United States of America.
First edition: 2021
10 9 8 7 6 5 4 3 2
ISBN: 978-1-947297-19-7 (trade paper)
ISBN: 978-1-947297-20-3 (eBook)

Publisher's Cataloging-in-Publication Data

Names: Epstein, Rhona, author.
Title: The satisfied workbook : a spiritual guide to recovery and food freedom / Dr. Rhona Epstein, PSY.D.
Description: Includes bibliographical references. | Nashville, TN: Dexterity, LLC, 2021.
Identifiers: ISBN: 9781947297197 (pbk.) | 9781947297203 (ebook)
Subjects: LCSH Weight loss—Religious aspects—Christianity. | Twelve-step programs—Religious aspects—Christianity. | Compulsive eating. | Food habits. | Eating disorders. | Weight loss—Psychological aspects. | Self-esteem. | Self-acceptance. | BISAC SELF-HELP / Eating Disorders & Body Image | RELIGION / Christian Living / Personal Growth
Classification: LCC RC552.C65 E7 2020 | DDC 616.85/26--dc23

Book design by Sarah Siegand. Cover design by Bruce Gore and Sarah Siegand.

To anyone willing to go to any length to experience freedom from an unhealthy relationship with food—blessings as you take your steps to peace with food and your body.

ALL THINGS ARE POSSIBLE WITH GOD.

The Twelve Steps

Step One

We admitted we were powerless over food—that our lives had become unmanageable.

Step Two

Came to believe that a Power greater than ourselves could restore us to sanity.

Step Three

Made a decision to turn our will and our lives over to the care of God as we understood Him.

Step Four

Made a searching and fearless moral inventory of ourselves.

Step Five

Admitted to God, to ourselves, and to another human being the exact nature of our wrongs.

Step Six

Were entirely ready to have God remove all these defects of character.

Step Seven

Humbly asked God to remove our shortcomings.

Step Eight

Made a list of all persons we had harmed and became willing to make amends to them all.

Step Nine

Made direct amends to such people wherever possible,
except when to do so would injure them or others.

Step Ten

Continued to take personal inventory and when we were wrong promptly admitted it.

Step Eleven

Sought through prayer and meditation to improve our conscious contact with God, as we understood Him, praying only for knowledge of His will for us and the power to carry that out.

Step Twelve

Having had a spiritual awakening as a result of these Steps, we tried to carry this message to other overeaters and to practice these principles in all our affairs.

CONTENTS

INTRODUCTION

Food addiction, eating disorders, and body dysmorphia are daunting problems to overcome. For those who don't struggle with these issues, it may seem that food and weight shouldn't wreak such havoc, yet so many of us are in bondage and unable to free ourselves!

Maybe that is where you find yourself today? I've been there too.

The diets just aren't working, your therapy isn't enough, medication hasn't fixed you, the fancy brand-name programs aren't doing it, and even prayer and Bible study don't seem to be cutting it.

Regardless of our efforts to change, our problem still feels insurmountable.

Back in the 1930s, a group of alcoholics faced the same challenges we face. They just couldn't get sober until they formed Alcoholics Anonymous and began to practice what is now known as the 12 Steps. (Now, these steps were originally derived from a Christian program, but the language of the steps was secularized for the sake of reaching all people.)

Since that time, the 12 Steps have been used by countless groups to overcome addictions, compulsions, or other behavioral problems that have not responded to other methods.

If this is your first introduction to them, you're probably wondering what is special about these 12 Steps? What do these steps have to do with your eating and weight issues? And these are excellent questions. At first glance, this workbook will seem to talk less about food and weight than other workbooks you may have tried.

You may even wonder, *Where are the dieting instructions located?*

Or, *Where is the chart that will tell me how many calories and fat grams I'm supposed to eat?*

Or, *What in the world does "making amends" have to do with the fact that I want to lose weight?*

It may not make sense right now, but stick with me. I promise, you will be glad you took the journey.

We are going to set out for something bigger than changing your calorie count. Working through these 12 Steps is a path of true change—inside-out change—and it is aimed at ending overeating. It isn't another quick-fix diet and exercise formula where you lose weight and gain it back (plus some).

This is an opportunity to focus on the transformation of your body, mind, and spirit. The process is aimed at eradicating the reasons you overeat, removing the baggage that fuels addiction and obsessive thinking. This experience will provide new ways of thinking and help you cultivate tools for taking control of your life so that you no longer use food as the drug to calm, strengthen, or manage your life.

The 12-Step process will help equip you to end addictive eating once and for all.

If you genuinely commit to this journey, you will recover and heal. You will find peace with food and your body. You will be in the right mindset about what you eat and how you look. Here's the caveat: The price tag for your freedom and peace is your total commitment to a painstaking process of **honesty** and **openness**. You need to be willing to seek God with all of your heart. You need to let go of self-destructive thinking, attitudes, habits, and relational patterns.

Remember this path is different. We are going for lasting lifelong change—ending the battle for good, learning to live free of the merry-go-round of diets and binges. If you're ready, I am here with you to lead the way. With God's help, your support system, and this guide, you will be directed step-by-step out of bondage into a life of peace and health with food and your body.

A few important matters we must address before we begin!

First, if you do not have a support system for food recovery, it is incredibly important that you get one. There are recovery groups for food addiction that are accessible either in person, online, or by phone. (Look up *Overeaters Anonymous* or *Full of Faith* to begin). Make sure to try different meetings and see what works best for you. You need people with whom you can connect as you go. Some of the steps will bring up difficult emotions, and you'll need other people to walk through them with you. Once your relationship with food is in good shape, use your support primarily for the emotional and spiritual aspects of your journey, and check in about food if a struggle arises.

Second, if you need help with food planning and accountability, it is essential to find the right person (or people) to assist you with finding the best plan for you. Everyone has different needs.

Third, be careful when you reach the more complicated steps that you stay the course. The steps will change your life for the better, but only if you do them. Remain steady and be patient with the experience, even though you will likely start to pull back at certain points. Try to do some work on your steps each week until you finish and try not to drag it out. Freedom comes later in the process, so you need to remember your goal: true freedom!

Throughout this workbook I have chosen to use the "we" pronoun at times as my inclusive calls to action. Why? Because, I have been right there in your shoes battling food addiction too (every day since 1981). I want to remind you that we are in this fight together. And no one can do this on their own! We recover with the help of others—often a team of support people. Never alone! Get used to that idea.

Finally, as you work through the issues that each step tackles, you will ultimately become adept at pinpointing what is fueling food thoughts and feelings, and you'll be equipped with better tools for handling each matter that arises. This process won't be easy at first… so be patient, and use your support!

Now, let's get started!

Dr. Rhona

STEP

One

ADMITTING DEFEAT

STEP ONE

Admitting Defeat

We admitted we were powerless over food—that our lives had become unmanageable.

For I know that nothing good dwells in me, that is, in my flesh.
For I have the desire to do what is right, but not the ability to carry it out.

ROMANS 7:18

OVERVIEW

Admitting and accepting powerlessness may sound easy enough. We can recognize the ways we've been unable to stop overeating on our own, that our problems with bingeing and weight keep getting worse regardless of repeated attempts to fix them. We must take an honest look at our relationship with food.

We may feel hopeless; maybe every previous attempt has created a feeling of utter failure. Maybe we are trapped in the cycle of performing the same destructive behaviors repeatedly: overeating, grazing all day, obsessing about food and weight, bingeing, hiding, sneaking, lying, pretending, dieting, exercising, hoping and losing hope, spending endless money on new programs, surgery, pills, gimmicks.

It's easy to say the words "I'm powerless. I know my strength has failed. I can't stop! I need help!" The challenge is to believe those words and allow that belief to change our actions. A person with a peanut allergy knows beyond a shadow of a doubt they are powerless over peanuts. They must go to great lengths to make sure they don't end up eating anything that has peanuts in it because it could be deadly. True awareness of powerlessness understands when something is deadly and what must be done to avoid it. When we truly face powerlessness over food, we should try to see the foods to which we are addicted (and the corresponding behaviors that activate that addiction) in the same way as the allergy sufferer sees peanuts. We must avoid all food and food behaviors that can trigger addiction. We need to know exactly what to do to stay safe with food at all times. Just as peanut allergies don't take vacations on holidays, neither do addictions.

The peanut allergy example is exactly the level of acceptance required to stop living in insanity and to quit activating the addiction by fueling it with toxic addictive foods and behaviors. Freedom comes with abstinence. Cravings dissipate when we don't feed our addiction.

In order to come to terms with this, it's helpful to take an honest look at what has really been happening in your relationship with food. The end of this step in the workbook will provide questions to help you examine what you eat, how you eat, how you get into trouble, what ways you have attempted to fix the problem, what helped, and what didn't. Please don't be discouraged. Having a clear picture of your out-of-control behavior and all its consequences will help you when you are tempted to pick up the first bite.

You might be unsure whether you have a food addiction and are, in fact, powerless. The best way to find out is to keep trying to control your eating. If you are able to control your portions and you have peace with food and your choices, you may not need to go through this process. But if you are taking quizzes to see if you are a food addict, chances are you need help. No one can make the determination if you need to go to the lengths of abstaining, support, and a twelve-step process but you. If you have been in a battle long enough, freedom may seem impossible, but many have been amazed at the miracles that come from taking this path.

Notes

Wendy was eager to resolve her problem with food and weight. She was on a weight loss journey and had hit a plateau when she started therapy. She was following a diet, and it was probably the tenth time she'd started a weight loss program. She was also once again at a place of losing control after losing a good amount of weight. When we examined her history, we found there was primarily a problem with sugary foods, especially chocolate. Bread and white flour products seemed to be the other area that got her into trouble. It took over a year for Wendy to face her addiction—to move from admitting her problem to accepting her powerlessness over it. Yes, she stayed current with food addiction literature, listened at meetings, and talked through the binges. But every time she was tempted, she had an excuse about why she thought it would be okay to just have one sweet at the church event, or the kid's birthday party, or the Christmas gathering. Each time was devastating and led to more and more trouble. Cravings, obsession, guilt, shame. It was never worth it, but it took some time to understand that sugar and white flour to Wendy were like alcohol to the alcoholic or drug to a drug addict.

Once she finally faced that she needed to be totally off all sugar and white flour, all cravings subsided and the fight with food ended. She was at peace with food. Leaving it alone was so much easier than trying to manage it. The power of addiction was too strong to fight. Freedom came for Wendy with *acceptance*, *surrender*, and *abstinence* from her addictive foods.

Wendy's story is so common. For me personally, it took 2.5 years of hard-core trying to quit overeating until I finally got it myself. I did everything right—I just could not understand the power of food addiction and the first bite until I did. Once I surrendered, the fight was over.

It's easy to believe we have taken step one because we can admit we have a problem. But most don't really accept powerlessness, and consequently, they never truly recover. Every time a person decides to have that first bite of whatever food takes them down the slippery slope of addictive eating, it's an indication they haven't yet faced powerlessness. When you understand the first bite will lead to the inability to stop, then you know there is no "I'll just have one" or "Tomorrow, I'll start my diet." A person who knows they are powerless knows one bite is never one bite—it is always the beginning of a loss of control that may take months or years to correct. If you are still sliding on the slippery slope of addictive eating, you still need to take the first step.

Focusing on You: EXAMINING YOUR HISTORY OF FOOD ADDICTION

YOUR PERSONAL FOOD STORY

Consider writing a thorough account of your relationship with food from the time you were young until today. This is an important project, and I don't want you to rush through it. You may choose to use a timeline format in chronological order of seasons of your life to help organize your thoughts and tell the story. (I have personally found writing your story as a timeline the most helpful way to see how the problem has manifested throughout your life. It helps to see similar patterns and themes in different situations and relationships).

You must go into the specific details, behaviors, and feelings about your eating, weight, and dieting. Discuss every area of your life that was impacted by your abnormal eating and obsession. Did you avoid people and activities because of your weight or because you were too hung over from binges? Did you create ways to get alone so you could eat without anyone knowing?

How were your relationships affected? Were you irritable or withdrawn? Did your shame cause you to pull away from important loved ones? Did you miss important aspects of your life because your head was so wrapped up in obsession that you missed what was going on? Did you hide, sneak, or lie? Did you steal? Did you act like everything was okay in front of people when you felt like dying inside from shame?

Be specific about what you were eating. How much? Did you eat in secret? What did you do to cover your tracks? Write about the diets. What did you do to try to control your eating and weight? How did it go? Were you obsessed with the scale? Did you ever experience freedom from cravings? Peace with food? What specific life events do you believe fueled your eating? Death? Loss? Certain stresses? What are your triggers? Who are your triggers?

Use the space on the following pages to reflect on these questions and write out your personal food story.

My Personal Food Story

_____

_____

_____

_____

_____

_____

_____

_____

_____

_____

_____

_____

_____

_____

_____

_____

_____

_____

_____

_____

_____

_____

_____

_____

_____

_____

_____

_____

_____

_____

_____

_____

_____

_____

Now that you have thoroughly looked at your dysfunctional relationship with food and grappled with the concept of powerlessness, let's answer some questions about your ability (or lack thereof) to control your eating.

RECOVERY QUESTIONS

1. Do you believe you can control your eating without help? Why?

   _____

   _____

2. Do you believe you are addicted to certain foods (meaning, every time you start eating certain foods you can't stop)? Discuss.

   _____

   _____

   _____

3. Do you think you can have just one bite? One cookie? One small dish of ice cream? Explain.

   _____

   _____

   _____

4. How do diets and weight control methods contribute to your overeating problem? Do you eat because of restriction? Do you reward yourself or overeat because you are hungry from missing meals? Discuss.

   _____

   _____

   _____

5. Do you recognize your life has become unmanageable? How?

   _____

   _____

   _____

6. Can you see how food abuse is robbing you of health, peace, sane thinking, clear thinking? Explain.

_____

_____

_____

_____

7. Do you believe that your food addiction will get better on its own? Why?

_____

_____

_____

_____

8. Addiction is a progressive illness—it's a problem that typically worsens if it is not treated. Has this been true for you? Do you see an increase of symptoms over time and a growing inability to get into control? Explain.

_____

_____

_____

_____

_____

YOUR STEP ONE CHALLENGE

Denial is the inability to see a problem clearly. Usually when a food addict is in denial, they are still trying to control their eating despite repeated failures. They have not come to a place of accepting the truth that when it comes to food, something is gravely wrong and intervention is needed. Throwing a little effort at fixing an addiction is like throwing a stone in the ocean. It makes no real impact. When a person realizes this is a real addiction that needs to be treated, they will then be willing to go to the lengths necessary to change and heal. That said, are you ready to face your food problem head-on?

What do you believe you need at this time to help make the changes to a life of sobriety with food?

- ☐ Food plan
- ☐ Nutritionist
- ☐ Counselor
- ☐ Treatment
- ☐ 12 step group
- ☐ Sponsor

What are you willing to do to get started?

STEP ONE
Scripture Meditations

Write out how each verse applies to you. What does it mean to you? How does it relate to your situation?

Matthew 26:41

The spirit indeed is willing, but the flesh is weak.

John 5:6

When Jesus saw him lying there and knew that he had already been there a long time, he said to him, "Do you want to be healed?"

Romans 5:6

For while we were still weak, at the right time Christ died for the ungodly.

1 Corinthians 8:2

If anyone imagines that he knows something, he does not yet know as he ought to know.

Romans 7:18-20

For I know that nothing good dwells in me, that is, in my flesh. For I have the desire to do what is right, but not the ability to carry it out. For I do not do the good I want, but the evil I do not want is what I keep on doing. Now if I do what I do not want, it is no longer I who do it, but sin that dwells within me.

2 Corinthians 12:9-10

"My grace is sufficient for you, for my power is made perfect in weakness." . . . For when I am weak, then I am strong.

BUILDING FAITH

STEP TWO

Building Faith

Came to believe that a Power greater than ourselves could restore us to sanity.

All things are possible for one who believes.
MARK 9:23

OVERVIEW

You have now come to understand that you are powerless over food, which presents a new question: Where does the power to overcome your addiction come from? The answer to that question is the foundation of your whole recovery journey and will finally relieve you of trying to make this problem go away on your own. There is a Power greater than you—this is good news! And He is the only way to restore your sanity. Are you ready to know God like you've never known Him before?

Before you answer that question, consider this one: Do you really trust that God is good? Plenty of people have trouble embracing God at all. I know I did before I started my recovery journey; God seemed remote and untouchable to me. In a world filled with suffering, injustice, and painful experiences, the idea of God can feel anywhere from insufficient to unfair. How can a good God not end suffering and pain? Why would He allow horrible things to happen to people, often leading them to food abuse in the first place? On the other hand, it is easy to feel guilty asking God for help with food abuse in the midst of war and famine. What place do I have asking God for help when people are dying from hunger? I should be able to take care of this myself!

Doubt can be a hindrance to faith building and, thus, recovery. Years of failures, sickness, losses, and trauma. Some things we can't explain or understand, but believing requires putting doubt

14

aside, even with our unanswered questions. The best defense against doubt is focusing on God's track record—it is one of love, power, healing, hope, strength, and victory. Even so, some days, you'll have to act as if you believe or "fake it till you make it!" It's part of the process. It is a daily practice to choose His grace over your shame. As you do, you will begin to believe that His power in you will do what you could never do all on your own. Your struggle will end when you learn to put the battle into His capable hands.

| The best defense against doubt is focusing on God's track record—it is one of love, power, healing, hope, strength, and victory.

The gospel teaches that Jesus died for us while we were still a mess and whether or not we could embrace Him. He will meet you right where you are, even if you're knee deep in pizza, ice cream, cookies, resistance, and confusion. In Romans 5:8, the apostle Paul wrote, "But God shows his love for us in that while we were still sinners, Christ died for us." He loves you no matter what! Stop for a second right now and wrap your head around that. This principle is so important to understand to be able to make real progress. God is approachable no matter your situation. His grace is sufficient. He entered a broken world as a human being, just like you, so He could deliver you from your pain. Who could possibly understand you better? There is no problem too small, no issue unworthy of His attention and care (see Matthew 6:26).

Begin the practice of saying this truth to yourself throughout each day. Make it your prayer: I can do all things in Him who gives me strength!

Notes

Jordan was raised with religion and attended church regularly. She had no problem with the idea of believing in God for help, but it wasn't until her sponsor gave her the assignment to pray each day for her recovery and to read and write about a couple of spiritual readings related to recovery that she began to see change in her ability to achieve sustainable recovery. She told me the lights came on, and suddenly, she was able to see how the spiritual connection worked to heal her food problem. In my own recovery, I have personally prayed for another day of freedom each and every day since my first steps in 1981, and I continue to acknowledge the truth that my new life is the Lord's work in me. When I first started, I had no faith at all. At that time, I tried prayer and faith because nothing else worked, and I had nothing to lose. I believe with all my heart that my recovery is a miracle. This is my prayer each morning before breakfast: "Lord, thank You for this day and for the freedom I have in You. Please keep me free today from compulsive overeating and obsessive thinking about food and my body size. Amen."

So many people are believers who love and know the Lord, but don't really believe He will help them in this area of food and weight. I want to encourage you no matter where you are in your spiritual journey to put all your experiences aside and come to God with an open heart and mind. My experience as a counselor has taught me that our hearts and misconceptions about God can often keep us from having the spiritual experience we need and desire. Sometimes these hurts and misconceptions are passed to us from the people who are supposed to love us, like our family.

It is important to start fresh with God around your recovery, but don't be afraid to take your grief, doubt, or confusion with you—He can handle it. You can never really know the heart of God or the freedom He offers without first being honest with Him. Identify the hurts and experiences that may keep you from trusting the Lord to be a force of love, power, healing, and strength, and give those feelings to Him. Spend time looking up the hundreds of verses in Scripture about God's love and favor. Read and re-read the story of the prodigal son (Luke 15:11-32) or the woman caught in adultery (John 8:1-11). Think about the nature of a God who has that kind of unconditional love and mercy for you. You are His child. Can you believe in that kind of grace and love?

RECOVERY QUESTIONS

1. Do you often feel out of control when it comes to food and weight? How so?

_____

_____

2. In what ways has your life been insane? Describe.

_____

_____

_____

3. Can you acknowledge that you need help from a power greater than yourself? Discuss.

_____

_____

4. What do you believe about who God is?

_____

_____

_____

5. What parental or authority figure projections might you be making on to God that limit your ability to see His grace and love? Do you assume He is like authority figures from your childhood rather than who you read about in Scripture? Are there other people you have experienced as hypocrites, or otherwise spiritually "off", who have affected your own ability to believe? Think and write about this. How does this affect how you approach God?

_____

_____

_____

6. Do you believe God can help you? Why? Why not?

_____

_____

_____

7. What faith practices have helped in the past?

_____

_____

_____

8. What faith practices have been harmful or useless?

_____

_____

_____

9. How has faith made a difference in your life?

_____

_____

_____

10. How does it affect you when you are not experiencing connection to God?

_____

_____

_____

YOUR STEP TWO CHALLENGE

Do you believe you can be free? If so, what do you imagine that would be like? Write about that. Use your imagination. If you were free . . .

Write five verses or phrases on which you can easily rely to help you remember to keep the faith and believe at all times.

1.

2.

3.

4.

5.

STEP TWO

Write out how each verse applies to you. What does it mean to you? How does it relate to your situation?

Mark 9:24

I believe; help my unbelief.

Luke 8:43-48

And there was a woman who had had a discharge of blood for twelve years, and though she had spent all her living on physicians, she could not be healed by anyone. She came up behind him and touched the fringe of his garment, and immediately her discharge of blood ceased. And Jesus said, "Who was it that touched me?" When all denied it, Peter said, "Master, the crowds surround you and are pressing in on you!" But Jesus said, "Someone touched me, for I perceive that power has gone out from me." And when the woman saw that she was not hidden, she came trembling, and falling down before him declared in the presence of all the people why she had touched him, and how she had been immediately healed. And he said to her, "Daughter, your faith has made you well; go in peace."

John 8:32

And you will know the truth, and the truth will set you free.

Hebrews 11:1-10

Now faith is the assurance of things hoped for, the conviction of things not seen. For by it the people of old received their commendation. By faith we understand that the universe was created by the word of God, so that what is seen was not made out of things that are visible. By faith Abel offered to God a more acceptable sacrifice than Cain, through which he was commended as righteous, God commending him by accepting his gifts. And through his faith, though he died, he still speaks. By faith Enoch was taken up so that he should not see death, and he was not found, because God had taken him. Now before he was taken, he was commended as having pleased God. And without faith it is impossible to please him, for whoever would draw near to God must believe that he exists and that he rewards those who seek him. By faith Noah, being warned by God concerning events as yet unseen, in reverent fear constructed an ark for the saving of his household. By this he condemned the world and became an heir of the righteousness that comes by faith. By faith Abraham obeyed when he was called to go out to a place that he was to receive as an inheritance. And he went out, not knowing where he was going. By faith he went to live in the land of promise, as in a foreign land, living in tents with Isaac and Jacob, heirs with him of the same promise. For he was looking forward to the city that has foundations, whose designer and builder is God.

2 Corinthians 3:5

Not that we are sufficient in ourselves to claim anything as coming from us, but our sufficiency is from God.

Philippians 4:13

I can do all things through him who strengthens me.

Isaiah 41:10

Fear not, for I am with you; be not dismayed, for I am your God; I will strengthen you, I will help you, I will uphold you with my righteous right hand.

STEP

Three

SURRENDERING TO GOD

STEP THREE

Surrendering to God

> **Made a decision to turn our will and our lives over to the care of God as we understood Him.**

I appeal to you therefore, brothers, by the mercies of God, to present your bodies as a living sacrifice, holy and acceptable to God, which is your spiritual worship.

ROMANS 12:1

OVERVIEW

Step 3 is about learning complete reliance and dependence on God. We may have a negative reaction to the idea of dependence on anyone. Maybe for good reason! Perhaps we have been hurt or let down, and trust is difficult. Or maybe it's simply a difficult concept to grasp. If we can't see or touch God, how do we depend on Him? Once we've considered God's character in Step 2, we understand He is a loving, unchangeable force; an unconditional safe haven; a refuge and a fortress; all-wise, all-loving, never-failing; and right there with you at all times.

Now let me challenge you that the lowercase "god" on whom you have been depending has failed you thus far. And if you don't think you've been dependent on anything or anyone, let's look a little closer at your relationship with food. Have you not turned to food for many of the things in life that God might have helped you with? Has food not been your comfort when God says He is the source of comfort? Have you not reached for food when you were stressed or frustrated instead of looking to Him for wisdom? Have you not eaten over relational conflicts instead of facing your troubles with His wisdom, strength, and courage? Now, it's time to challenge this unhealthy dependence and switch it out for a dependence that will work to bring health, sanity, and peace.

It's one thing to pray, attend worship services, read Scripture, participate in recovery groups, engage in charitable giving, help in ministries or service positions, or any other number of activities around spiritual life. It's an entirely different matter to fully surrender your life to your Creator. The concept of surrender is not easily understood. What does it mean to turn your life over to God? How is it done?

Alcoholics Anonymous literature explains that the effectiveness of the entire 12 Step Program depends on how willing you are to turn your life over to God. That should make you pause and think about the importance of this step. Remember what we already know: Our way doesn't work—all the diets, weight focus, and attempts at control have left us in a mess. So, if the idea of trusting God is tough for you, let me challenge you to consider this: What do you have to lose?

Surrender requires total trust, and trust means accepting help. Trusting the process of healing is a form of surrender itself. I believe God is at work in these methods, evident in the hundreds of thousands of people all over the world who have been set free using twelve-step programs. The term in AA literature is "desperate dependence." You must understand the choice—it's either God or food addiction. You can't have both. When you choose addiction, you brush God aside. When you focus on God's love, presence, and power, your shame and self-reliance will be replaced with the freedom His truth brings. It may seem counterintuitive, but in seeking dependence on Him, you are set free.

So, trust. Get up each day, and commit to following through with the tools of a food plan, support calls, the steps, and meetings. Surrender is a daily choice, just like any other component of your journey to healing.

Notes

My friend, Arielle, was an active member of her church. She was a great dieter who lost weight by closely following plans, but she could never seem to stay on track. She started therapy and a twelve-step group. Arielle attended meetings and found it all to be quite helpful. Unfortunately, the struggle continued until she started to work her steps. She learned some big lessons about surrender and depending on God in her step three readings. As she developed a new childlike dependence on God (that was less "works"-related and more faith-based), she began to experience the Lord's power working in her, enabling her to let go of the food and unhealthy behaviors and attitudes so that she could live in God's love in freedom.

In Step 2 we decided to truly believe in God, and now we take another big step to practice dependence on God. I personally found this step quite challenging. I didn't understand how to depend on something I couldn't see or touch. I spent a lot of time considering how to surrender. I still do. It's perplexing. Isaiah 40:31 reads, "They shall mount up with wings like eagles; they shall run and not be weary; they shall walk and not faint." As I let myself imagine the concept of being on the wings of an eagle, I begin to understand what it means to be carried by the Lord's power. Faith is believing in Someone I can't see or comprehend. Trust is giving my life over. Faith and trust work—even if I don't understand why!

Think of trusting God like electricity. Imagine that you have a super high-tech, high-capacity computer. Imagine all the possibilities of what you may be able to do with your computer. There is one small problem: It needs electricity to work. If you don't plug it in, it really doesn't matter how high the capacity is. We are the same way. When we are not plugged in to God, we don't work well. Junk food and excess food are false forms of energy! When we look to the wrong thing for sustenance, it eventually turns our lives upside down. Trusting God means we are plugging into the Power source! He provides the energy we need to be healthy and functional in every area of our lives.

The more we choose to practice trust and allow our hearts and our spirits to be fed by God, the more equipped we will be to live the life we have always wanted. I can't encourage you enough: Make the Lord first, and feed on His Word. Choose surrender; allow yourself to be surprised by what you didn't think was possible: freedom.

RECOVERY QUESTIONS

1. What do you believe it means to turn your life and will over to the care of God?

   _____

   _____

2. What are you willing to turn over to God?

   _____

   _____

3. What are you holding back from Him? How does holding back areas of your life from God affect you?

   _____

   _____

4. What is holding you back from letting go and letting God have it all?

   _____

   _____

5. What are you afraid of?

   _____

   _____

6. How has your relationship with food been a form of dependence? How have you turned to food when you might have turned to the Lord? Write all the examples you can think of how food was a god.

   _____

   _____

   _____

YOUR STEP THREE CHALLENGE

How do you envision your life with God in control? Write out your mental picture: If I were trusting in the Lord and leaning on Him . . .

We have worn ourselves out trying to fix our problems with our own strength. We are exhausted from the obsession and the constant negotiations/food fights in our heads. Other areas of our lives have suffered as well. We don't have the strength to manage this on our own. But, God calls us to bring it all to Him. Write down examples of times you have depended on the Lord. How has that worked out?

Today, practice praying these words, "Dear God, I am trusting You with my life today."

STEP THREE

Write out how each verse applies to you. What does it mean to you? How does it relate to your situation?

Philippians 1:6

And I am sure of this, that he who began a good work in you will bring it to completion at the day of Jesus Christ.

Deuteronomy 30:15-20

See, I have set before you today life and good, death and evil. If you obey the commandments of the Lord your God that I command you today, by loving the Lord your God, by walking in his ways, and by keeping his commandments and his statutes and his rules, then you shall live and multiply, and the Lord your God will bless you in the land that you are entering to take possession of it. But if your heart turns away, and you will not hear, but are drawn away to worship other gods and serve them, I declare to you today, that you shall surely perish. You shall not live long in the land that you are going over the Jordan to enter and possess. I call heaven and earth to witness against you today, that I have set before you life and death, blessing and curse. Therefore choose life, that you and your offspring may live, loving the Lord your God, obeying his voice and holding fast to him, for he is your life and length of days, that you may dwell in the land that the Lord swore to your fathers, to Abraham, to Isaac, and to Jacob, to give them.

Ephesians 5:18

And do not get drunk with wine, for that is debauchery, but be filled with the Spirit.

Psalm 46:1

God is our refuge and strength, a very present help in trouble.

Proverbs 3:5-6

Trust in the LORD with all your heart and do not lean on your own understanding. In all your ways acknowledge him, and he will make straight your paths.

Matthew 11:28-30

Come to me, all who labor and are heavy laden, and I will give you rest. Take my yoke upon you, and learn from me, for I am gentle and lowly in heart, and you will find rest for your souls. For my yoke is easy, and my burden is light.

Isaiah 40:31

But they who wait for the LORD shall renew their strength; they shall mount up with wings like eagles; they shall run and not be weary; they shall walk and not faint.

James 4:7-10

Submit yourselves therefore to God. Resist the devil, and he will flee from you. Draw near to God, and he will draw near to you. Cleanse your hands, you sinners, and purify your hearts, you double-minded. Be wretched and mourn and weep. Let your laughter be turned to mourning and your joy to gloom. Humble yourselves before the Lord, and he will exalt you.

2 Corinthians 5:17

Therefore, if anyone is in Christ, he is a new creation. The old has passed away; behold, the new has come.

Isaiah 54:4-8

"Fear not, for you will not be ashamed; be not confounded, for you will not be disgraced . . . but with everlasting love I will have compassion on you," says the LORD, your Redeemer.

STEP
Four

SEARCHING OURSELVES

STEP FOUR

Searching Ourselves

Made a searching and fearless moral inventory of ourselves.

Search me, O God, and know my heart! Try me and know my thoughts! And see if there be any grievous way in me, and lead me in the way everlasting.

Psalm 139:23-24

OVERVIEW

What does a moral inventory have to do with my food and weight issues? I've seen so many people glance at the steps, notice this one, and decide a twelve-step program isn't for them. There will probably be so many moments during this step at which point you'll ask yourself: Why do I have to do this? Just remember that this is an awesome opportunity for you to get rid of the underlying emotional and spiritual issues behind your eating. It is part of a process of true inside-out change.

Now isn't the time to quit! Just because this step may seem daunting, that doesn't make it something to run away from. The end of cravings, obsession, and insanity with food and weight depends in part on going through this self-exploration. Breathe, pray, stay close to your supports, and do it! Don't put it off.

In this step, we will discuss how to conduct a complete and thorough personal inventory of yourself. We will look at your character strengths and weaknesses, your secret shames and your gifts and blessings. It's necessary to be thorough and honest. Although this guide will give you plenty of questions as prompts, you may not identify with all of them (but don't be discouraged if you can). Take time to think about the questions.

I have to be honest with you—this step is likely to be really tough. It's easy to pretend that you only have a food and weight problem and that these other issues don't really relate until you get honest and pull away the layers of denial. Don't be afraid. Don't try to cover up. Just be open, look in, and let the Lord show you so you can have a clean house—and remove the fuel for food abuse and cravings.

Everyone develops character strengths and weaknesses in relation to their own life experiences. Some of the ways we develop can become maladaptive, or not conducive to adapting well, but they also work for our survival. We learn from people and experiences and create coping strategies to function. But many of these strategies can be extremely unhealthy and cause inner turmoil or relational conflict. Even our addictive eating is a coping strategy that we have learned to shield and protect us from painful emotions we weren't prepared to manage. Yes, the food softened the agony of life for a time, until it became part of the problem.

We have used our character defects to protect us in an unsafe world. Here we will uncover the truth and eventually come to a place of inviting God and our support system to help us keep what is best and let go of what is unhealthy and destructive. This step is intense, so take your time. Remember these rules: Don't worry or judge yourself harshly, just focus on being honest and transparent. Remember that God is walking through this with you! He is holding you by the hand, and He will neither leave you nor forsake you (see Deuteronomy 31:6). You are already forgiven. Consider this part of the process, just like cleaning house! We are going to get rid of stuff that is long overdue for removal. So, roll up your sleeves, and let's do this.

Notes

Jessie was a bit of a perfectionist. When she was presented with the different Step 4 methods, she became obsessed with picking "the right one," so she would be sure to get it correct. She started one path that a friend suggested, but then thought she might not be doing it right. She then looked to another option. She was so concerned with the method and process and getting it perfect that she missed the point: Get the inventory done. Jessie needed permission to do an imperfect inventory. She needed to take a plunge, pick a path, be honest, and just go with it. By working through this tough step, she also learned to let others help her and to lighten up on herself. She completed the step by focusing on letting go of perfection!

Honestly, Step 4 is where I've seen more people crash on their recovery than any other. I've learned through many years of counseling how easy it is to get caught up in some form of perfectionism and just quit. In my Step 4, I had so much self-hate that I was eager to write all about my defects of character. I kept looking because I was sure I was the worst and there was no end to the defects. I had difficulty finding any strengths, and I had trouble moving on. Step 4 can be a daunting process, so it is important to take your time, be patient, and go easy with it. It can also be scary to bring up things that you may rather keep buried. So, I do not suggest going back into past issues you've already resolved. Only jump into the areas where you feel there is unfinished business. But also remember, just like house cleaning, some areas need more than one good solid scrub. Also, we have practiced avoidance for a good reason—these memories can be unpleasant. So, it's necessary to trust God and your support people as you go through this process.

Remember: You are ridding the fuel for addictive eating from your house. This is a worthwhile project. You may not like it while you do it, but you will love it when it's done. These agonizing old issues will no longer run your life.

Before we go any further, let's pause and pray!

Heavenly Father, please help me to take this next step with You. Help me to not be fearful and to take one section at a time holding Your hand, experiencing Your sweet Spirit close to me. Thank You, Lord, that I am not alone. Thank You ahead of time for the healing You are doing through this process. Thank You that there is no condemnation for those who trust in You. Thank You that You are happy to hear my confession and take away each and every one of my troubles. In Jesus' name. Amen.

Out of necessity, the arrangement of this chapter is much different than the first three steps. Some of the inventory questions will take some time to get through, so try not to approach too much in one sitting. There are Scriptures in this chapter that are paired with the longer inventory sections, and I have added some quotes that have meant something to me in my own journey to help you through those moments of reflection. Some of the inventories are short and will require only a couple answers! Take your time and be honest.

Now we can get down to work:

1. Is there anything keeping you from taking your fourth step and writing your searching and fearless moral inventory?

2. What do you need to help you successfully complete this challenging step?

3. What is the best plan for following through with making regular time to write out your inventory until it is complete?

ANGER

Be angry and do not sin; do not let the sun go down on your anger.

Ephesians 4:26

Know this, my beloved brothers: let every person be quick to hear, slow to speak, slow to anger.

James 1:19

Internalizing anger will take away our joy and spirit; externalizing anger will make us less effective in our attempts to create change and forge connection. It's an emotion that we need to transform into something life-giving: courage, love, change, compassion, justice. Or sometimes anger can mask a far more difficult emotion like grief, regret, or shame, and we need to use it to dig into what we're really feeling. Either way, anger is a powerful catalyst but a life-sucking companion.

—Brené Brown[1]

Anger is one of those often-challenging emotional experiences that can be so uncomfortable we become quick to shut it down. Whether we are afraid to explode and hurt someone or say the wrong thing and possibly cause upset, many of us have never learned to deal with these strong emotions appropriately. Sadly, food has been the way we have managed, and it has worked to shut down those intense feelings. We need to find another way. We need to learn to say what we mean without being mean. We need to learn to process our feelings with God's help and our supports.

Let's talk about anger:

Make a list of all the people with whom you are angry and why.

How is your anger typically expressed?

Give examples of holding anger in or suppressing anger.

Give examples of inappropriate outward expression of anger.

How would you rate your ability to express anger appropriately?

Do you have awareness of misdirected anger, such as taking out your anger or frustration on people or animals? Have you ever been abusive?

How have you been angry at yourself? How does that play out in your thoughts? Actions?

ANXIETY

Do not be anxious about anything, but in everything by prayer and supplication with thanksgiving let your requests be made known to God.

PHILIPPIANS 4:6

Do not be anxious, saying, "What shall we eat?" or "What shall we drink?" or "What shall we wear?" For the Gentiles seek after all these things, and your heavenly Father knows that you need them all. But seek first the kingdom of God and his righteousness, and all these things will be added to you. Therefore do not be anxious about tomorrow, for tomorrow will be anxious for itself. Sufficient for the day is its own trouble.

MATTHEW 6:31-34

_____

There's a reason the Bible speaks so eloquently and frequently about confronting anxiety—even the strongest believers come up against it. It can be vague and a general state of being or set off by certain life factors. Ask for peace from the Lord as you work through your specific anxieties.

Let's talk about anxiety:

Do you struggle with anxiety—social anxiety, performance anxiety, general anxiety, or a specific phobia? What are you anxious about? Describe.

How have you already tried to work on your anxiety issues?

How does food tie into your anxiety issues?

Has anxiety been a problem since childhood?

APPROVAL SEEKING

For am I now seeking the approval of man, or of God? Or am I trying to please man? If I were still trying to please man, I would not be a servant of Christ.

GALATIANS 1:10

Beware of practicing your righteousness before other people in order to be seen by them.

MATTHEW 6:1

———————————

There is nothing wrong with wanting to be liked or behaving in a way that considers others before ourselves. But things get messy when we are acting out of fear of rejection and a desire for validation instead of selfless love and a desire to be like Jesus.

Let's talk about approval seeking:

Do you fear criticism or disapproval? Discuss.

Are you constantly seeking validation?

Have you lost your sense of your own wants and needs in living to be liked by others? Discuss.

Are you making up for validation you never received as a child by doing all you can to always be validated now?

What is the price you are paying for your life of approval seeking?

BITTERNESS AND RESENTMENT

Strive for peace with everyone, and for the holiness without which no one will see the Lord.
HEBREWS 12:14

It is forgiveness alone that has the capacity to break the chains of injustice
and give us the possibility of a new future—a future unchained from the past and free of bitterness.
The world of resentment and bitterness is a small, ever-shrinking world.
—BRIAN ZAHND[2]

Resentment is the number one offender—it kills more alcoholics than anything else.
—AA BIG BOOK[3]

———————————

Resentment is nursed anger. It's the refusal to let go and a hurt or offense remains unresolved, buried—when it grows and has roots and becomes almost a part of you. One of the earmarks of addiction is the tendency to blame others, the world, and circumstances for our troubles. We sit, eating out of control, complaining about how badly the world has treated us. We used to say in addiction treatment, "When you have one finger pointing out, there are three pointing back at you." The 12 Step philosophy is meant to help you find a way to take your eyes off what is wrong with others and the world and do something about yourself. It's good to allow some grief over painful realities, but you aren't supposed to live there. To be able to recover, you need to find a way to heal the hurts—or even learn to live with them, but not have them in the driver's seat of your heart and mind.

Let's talk about bitterness and resentment:

Who do you resent? Make a list.

As you look at your list, what are the themes? What are your buttons? Your relational vulnerabilities? Have you tried to get others back? In what way?

What's the issue? What's your part? How are you hurt? What are the underlying issues? *Wounded self-esteem, fear of abandonment, selfish ambitions or desires, security, jealousy . . .*

Has bitterness impacted your mood? Your relationships with people?

How does your resentment tie into your dysfunctional use of food?

Can you see your part? What are you learning about yourself? Can you see how you've been hurt and what you might need besides food?

CHILDHOOD TRAUMA

You have kept count of my tossings; put my tears in your bottle. Are they not in your book?
PSALM 56:8

He will wipe away every tear from their eyes, and death shall be no more, neither shall there be mourning, nor crying, nor pain anymore, for the former things have passed away.
REVELATION 21:4

———————————

Childhood trauma can include the byproducts of many things: alcoholism, anger, rage, divorce, sexual abuse, bullying, neglect, emotional abuse. We are all someone's child, and despite our parents' best efforts (or lack thereof) many of us do not reach adulthood without significant hurt that is sometimes so deep we fear it can never be healed.

Food is often the first source of comfort for these painful experiences, which explains why food abuse often begins at a young age. We cannot hope for true recovery and, therefore, freedom without first turning to our potentially painful pasts. Our deeper wounds may seem to be buried in the past, but if they are unhealed, they are likely still the source of current emotional and relational reactions. There is absolutely no need to minimize something incredibly painful that happened when you were a child simply because you are now an adult and "should be over it."

Sometimes without realizing it, we keep our pain buried with food, because that's what we've been doing since the wound was initially inflicted. If bingeing and food abuse have always been our source of comfort, removing them will naturally bring to the surface what we have done our best to forget. Have grace on yourself: You were simply trying to take care of yourself in a way that was accessible. But you don't need to embrace unhealthy behaviors anymore to numb the pain.

The Lord will carry you through the darkest valley into quiet places free of suffering. He wants you to be well, and He will never forsake you.

Let me reiterate: If your inventory is bringing to light unhealed trauma from your childhood, PLEASE don't feel you need to handle it on your own! Lean into your support team. Seek out a qualified therapist. Take as much time as you need to address this issue. You've probably been carrying it with you for the majority of your life, so give yourself the appropriate time and care to heal.

Let's talk about childhood trauma:

Are there any traumatic events or experiences from your childhood that you feel have not completely healed?

Are there any that you feel have not been addressed at all? Describe them.

If you did not have a major experience of abuse or abandonment in childhood, what was your experience of criticism or rejection?

What was your social experience as a child? Did you experience any rejection or bullying?

Were your parents emotionally neglectful, too demanding? What were your reactions at the time?

How have these patterns played out in your relationships with your parents as an adult? (Give as many examples and details as you can remember.)

Were you ever put into any inappropriate sexual situations as a child? Not necessarily abuse, but asked a question by an adult, accidentally saw something inappropriate, etc.? How did this affect you and your relationship to sexuality?

DENIAL

Whoever conceals his transgressions will not prosper, but he who confesses
and forsakes them will obtain mercy.

PROVERBS 28:13

Pretending everything is okay while knowing you're a mess can be exhausting. It's difficult to tell the truth about food abuse. Shame and guilt over the loss of control can keep you hiding the problem so that no one ever knows the real story. There's just one issue: You know. Deep down inside is a place that desperately needs help and healing. We are only as sick as our secrets, and it is absolutely necessary to make a habit of truth telling if we are going to be free!

Let's talk about denial:

Give examples of how you have kept your food abuse a secret. Write honestly about what it feels like to pretend, live a double life, or act like all is well when in reality . . . it isn't.

How has that affected your relationship with God? With people? How does it affect the way you feel about yourself?

Peter again denied it, and at once a rooster crowed.

In the Gospel story of Peter, when Jesus predicted he would deny Him three times, Peter didn't even seem to be aware of his own weakness. He thought his love for Jesus was strong enough that he would never deny Him, but the Lord knew he was weak.

This example of denial is *extremely* powerful.

Can you recognize in your life how you have not been able to see your own weakness? How have you overestimated your faith or strength and assumed you were stronger and more together than you actually were?

Denial occurs when you don't even know and can't even see yourself accurately. Write about this regarding your relationship with food.

Do you tend to minimize your problems and act like they aren't really so bad, making light of things or even joking around? How so?

MORAL INVENTORY

Do you get angry when anyone catches you or comments on your eating, trying to get the attention off you and your behavior? Discuss.

Do you blame other people or circumstances for your eating rather than owning your problem? Why?

Do you avoid talking about subjects that might make you address the vulnerable truth about your eating and weight issues? Explain.

DEPENDENCE ON OTHERS

It is better to take refuge in the LORD than to trust in man.
PSALM 118:8

In the middle of our lives, we mistakenly fall prey to the myth that successful people
are those that help rather than need, and broken people need rather than help...
But the truth is that no amount of money, influence, resources, or determination will
change our physical, emotional, and spiritual dependence on others.
—BRENÉ BROWN[4]

People prone to addictions are likely to have more than one dependency. In my experience, counseling people with food issues, dependency issues and codependency most often go hand-in-hand. Once we begin to work through food abuse, people tend to begin to look for that "fix" from the object of their dependence. This can be a romantic relationship, a child, or a person in need because being needed often brings a powerful sense of well-being. This need to be loved, needed, or given attention is another fixation. Love and relationships are real needs, just like food is a real need for the body. But when we look for food or another person to fix what's broken inside, there's a problem. Many of the same characteristics of addiction can be seen in dependent or codependent relationships: obsession, loss of control, mood instability related to the object of dependence, and the negative impact on other areas of life.

Let's talk about dependence and codependence:

Do you worry endlessly about potentially being rejected?

How have you been dependent/addictive/obsessive or codependent in your relationships?

How is your dependency on others affecting your life?

How does your self-esteem relate to your dependent relationships?

What's the connection between food and addictive relationships?

Can you see how inner turmoil caused by these unhealthy relationships can keep you needing excess food to shut down the pain inside? Why?

DISHONESTY

For we aim at what is honorable not only in the Lord's sight but also in the sight of man.
2 Corinthians 8:21

Do not lie to one another, seeing that you have put off the old self with its practices.
Colossians 3:9

Whoever desires to love life and see good days, let him keep his tongue
from evil and his lips from speaking deceit.
1 Peter 3:10

———————————

Most of us have lied to ourselves and others about our eating: We have stolen and hidden food, and we have cheated on our diets. And after a while, we've found ourselves lying so much that we actually began to believe those lies. When we unpack our stories, we must be completely honest with ourselves. The shame of hiding and secrecy needs to be cleaned up; we need the grace of God to cover it all. Go back in your memory, and write all the incidences you can remember of lying, stealing, and cheating with food.

Let's talk about dishonesty:

Do you lie about your eating? Do you lie about your dieting? Explain.

Besides food, how else have you been dishonest in your life? Consider relationships, school, work, and finances. Make a list.

When have you found yourself stealing, lying, or cheating? How did it feel?

How does your dishonesty affect your relationships? Be specific about the affected relationships. How do you feel about your dishonest behavior?

FEAR

For God gave us a spirit not of fear but of power and love and self-control.
2 TIMOTHY 1:7

There is no fear in love; but perfect love casts out fear.
1 JOHN 4:18

*For I, the LORD your God, hold your right hand; it is I who say to you,
"Fear not, I am the one who helps you."*
ISAIAH 41:13

*Courage is not the absence of fear, but rather the assessment that
something else is more important than fear.*
–FRANKLIN D. ROOSEVELT[5]

———————————

Fear is one of the few universal emotions, and it's almost always coupled with worry. Fear can be paralyzing. It can keep us from fully living. It is found behind many other troubling areas in which we are honest with ourselves. Fear can limit our willingness to take risks, to love, to try new things, to experience the world. It can keep us from living to our fullest potential, from serving the Lord, from stepping out in our gifts. Fear can keep us in the food. We worry about rejection, and then we create self-fulfilling prophecies in which we set ourselves up for just that. Let's focus on what particular areas are consistently causing fear and worry in your life. Don't worry—you can do this!

Let's talk about fear and worry:

What are the things you usually worry about? Be specific—what are your concerns and how worried do you get? Do you obsess about these concerns?

What are your fears for the future? Elaborate on how much time and energy you spend on them.

How have you been afraid of people? Do you isolate out of fear? Do you eat instead of relate? How?

Are you afraid to reach out to others? Do you have trouble trusting others? How has that affected you?

Do you tend to people-please and not set boundaries because you are afraid of rejection or consequences? Discuss.

How has avoidance of expressing feelings related to your eating?

Are you conflict-avoidant? Do you accept unacceptable treatment rather than assertively set boundaries just because you are afraid of conflict? Explain.

Have you ended up in abusive relationships because of fear? Discuss.

Have you stayed in relationships, jobs, ministries, or groups for fear of doing what was best for you or not having the courage or ability to set boundaries?

How has fear held you back from following your dreams and seeking opportunities in work, ministry, love, or education?

Are you afraid of change? Give examples of situations you stayed in for fear of change.

Have you been afraid of certain people groups, such as certain racial groups, religions, institutions, demographics? Explain.

Overall, how have fear and anxiety led you to overeating?

FROZEN FEELINGS

Nothing is covered up that will not be revealed,
or hidden that will not be known.

LUKE 12:2

Getting out of your own way means being with who you are, moment to moment, whether you like
it or not. Whether or not it's easy or comfortable, familiar or disturbing.

–DENNIS PALUMBO[6]

One of the main reasons people develop an addictive relationship with food is to numb their emotions. Research has found that a good binge can create the same response as certain drugs when abused, which makes sense. No wonder we see people drowning themselves in mounds of ice cream after a breakup; it's either alcohol or ice cream! Both manage to create a numbing effect that temporarily push away unwanted emotions.

Unfortunately, when we learn to do this from a young age, we don't develop normal emotional coping skills, so we rely on staying numb as our only method for coping. This can lead to emotional immaturity and make us terrified to feel anything. But God has another idea about our feelings. In Scripture, we see God calling us to cast our cares on Him. We see people calling to Him in days of trouble. He says He is near to the brokenhearted, and He hears when we cry out to Him.

Let's talk about frozen feelings:

Are you aware of numbing out your feelings? Discuss.

Do you let yourself feel or do you do all that you can to put a stop to emotional discomfort?

Are you able to experience joyful or happy feelings, or are they numb as well?

Give examples of times you purposely used food to shut down your emotions.

Are there some feelings you are more likely to shove food at than others; for example, anger? Explain.

INSECURITY

For the LORD sees not as man sees: man looks on the outward appearance,
but the LORD looks on the heart.
1 SAMUEL 16:7

We all have our limitations, but when we listen to our critics, we also have theirs.
–ROBERT BRAULT[7]

Doubt kills more dreams than failure ever will.
–SUZY KASSEM[8]

———————————

For most of us, the insecurities list can be long: childhood rejection, feeling stupid in school, not being picked in gym class or not having the right friends or the right clothes, never completing college, not making enough money, etc. (It all sounds silly when we write it out, but our insecurities are no joke.) So many of us live with a constant sense of not feeling "okay" in the world. We walk around feeling like we just don't measure up—like somehow, we aren't enough. Weight might play a part in this, since being overweight tends to make us feel like we aren't okay. But insecurity can find its roots in many areas.

Let's talk about insecurities:

In what ways have you felt insecure? Give examples.

Where did that insecurity first begin?

How do you react to your insecurities?

List the ways your insecurities influence your behavior.

IRRESPONSIBILITY OR OVER-RESPONSIBILITY

Whatever you do, work heartily, as for the Lord and not for men.
COLOSSIANS 3:23

So whoever knows the right thing to do and fails to do it, for him it is sin.
JAMES 4:17

Problems arise when people act as if their "boulders" are daily loads, and refuse help, or as if their "daily loads" are boulders they shouldn't have to carry. The results of these two instances are either perpetual pain or irresponsibility.
–HENRY CLOUD[9]

_____

Some of us seem not to have an off button. We take on too much. We say "yes" when we know inside we should say "no." And then we get agitated on the inside with feelings that lead us to use food to quiet them.

On the other hand, there are those of us who tend to avoid responsibility. There may be myriad reasons behind that; perfectionism may lead you to do nothing for fear of not doing it "perfect enough." Laziness, fear, confusion, and simply not being able to ask for help can contribute to it as well.

Let's talk about irresponsibility and over-responsibility:

With which do you struggle more—being over-responsible or irresponsible?

What does that look like in your life? Is it tied to relationships, work, church, or other areas? (Think through and identify some recent examples.)

In what specific ways do you tend to be over-responsible?

How do you struggle with being irresponsible?

Do you wrestle with being a perfectionist? How does this impact you?

What about procrastination? Do you tend to put things that need to be done off till another day and then live with a to-do list that keeps growing? Discuss.

Do you procrastinate because of laziness? Because of over-committing yourself? Perhaps because of a lack of boundaries? For fear of failure? Because you think tasks are too difficult?

ISOLATION

Then the LORD God said, "It is not good that the man should be alone;
I will make him a helper fit for him."

GENESIS 2:18

And let us consider how to stir up one another to love and good works,
not neglecting to meet together, as is the habit of some, but encouraging one another,
and all the more as you see the Day drawing near.

HEBREWS 10:24-25

It is said addiction is a disease of isolation. It also is believed that the opposite of addiction is connection. For most of our lives, we have chosen food over love. We hid behind food rather than developing healthy emotionally intimate relationships. If we are being honest, we may find that we are afraid to be close, afraid of being rejected.

Let's talk about isolation:

How has self-isolation impacted your life?

How has this affected your family relationships?

How has this affected your friendships?

How has this affected your romantic relationships?

How has food been connected to your isolation tendencies?

JEALOUSY

A tranquil heart gives life to the flesh, but envy makes the bones rot.
PROVERBS 14:30

For love is strong as death, jealousy is fierce as the grave.
SONG OF SOLOMON 8:6

———————————

No matter how good we have it, there's always something someone else has that we don't. It's the human condition. This endless cycle of feeling like we don't have enough can easily translate into poor eating behaviors—we feel like we're lacking, so we desperately try to fill ourselves up. But the truth is, nothing can ever fully satisfy us but Jesus, no matter what we fantasize about or wish we had.

Let's talk about jealousy:

Of whom in your life, past or present, have you been jealous?

What attributes of their lives did you envy? Relationships, finances, lack of suffering, etc.? Are there any recurring themes?

Imagine your life with each of the things you listed that someone had, but you didn't. What would you lose about your life as it is? How does that make you feel?

How has jealousy affected your relationships? Have any relationships in your life ended because of jealousy?

How has jealousy affected your eating behaviors?

How do you think God's jealousy of us as His people in the Bible differs from your own human jealousy?

Is there any version of your life that you can think of that is "enough"? Discuss.

NEGATIVE THINKING

*We destroy arguments and every lofty opinion raised against the knowledge of God,
and take every thought captive to obey Christ.*

2 CORINTHIANS 10:5

If you believe that the world is conspiring against you, it will just do that.
—ANONYMOUS

———————————

Rewiring the way you think, especially surrounding negative thinking habits, is one of the most crucial aspects of your recovery. Most of us think we're set in our "thinking ways." But the Scripture above shows us that just isn't true—we must "take every thought captive"—and in that we find freedom. We can learn to choose what we think—to focus on what is good—and to shut down what is destructive and harmful. We do have a choice! We are not subject to our automatic negative thoughts.

Let's talk about negative thinking:

How does negative thinking affect your mood?

How often do you engage in negative thinking spirals? What are the typical focuses or themes of your negative thinking spirals?

How does negative thinking affect your eating? How does your eating affect your negative thinking? Can you see the connection?

What skills have you used to stop negative thinking, and how effective are they?

Are you able to take your thoughts captive as the Scripture says? Are you able to apply the Word in a helpful way? How?

PRIDE

Pride goes before destruction, and a haughty spirit before a fall.
PROVERBS 16:18

As long as you are proud you cannot know God. A proud man is always looking down on things and people; and, of course, as long as you are looking down, you cannot see something that is above you.
–C. S. LEWIS[10]

The proud person always wants to do the right thing, the great thing. But because he wants to do it in his own strength, he is fighting not with man, but with God.
–SØREN KIERKEGAARD[11]

———————————

It is one type of pride to experience a sense of accomplishment—to feel proud. It is a different thing to have false pride, which is more like arrogance—this is the pride the Scripture warns us about! Pride can keep us from getting the help we need. It is opposite of the position we need to take with God and the people we need for support. When we think we should be okay on our own and keep doing things in our own strength, we end up in trouble. If we protect ourselves from facing our inadequacy and weakness, we will never recover.

Let's talk about pride:

In what ways have you been prideful? How has arrogance characterized your behavior?

How has pride caused you to get into trouble? Give examples.

How has pride kept you from receiving help? Explain.

SELF-CARE

Do you not know that you are God's temple and that God's Spirit dwells in you?
1 Corinthians 3:16

Knowing how to be solitary is central to the art of loving. When we can be alone, we can be with others without using them as a means of escape.
—Bell Hooks[12]

Self-care is never a selfish act—it is simply good stewardship of the only gift I have, the gift I was put on earth to offer others. Anytime we can listen to true self and give the care it requires, we do it not only for ourselves, but for the many others whose lives we touch.
—Parker Palmer[13]

———————————

Do you tend to use food as the primary way to care for yourself? Sometimes when we overdo it by working too much, caregiving, socializing, saying "yes" when we mean "no," and not heeding our bodily cravings for rest, we can end up using food as our only form of self-care. What does that look like? Well, instead of giving ourselves a rest, we give ourselves food. Instead of time with a friend or loved one, we spend time with food. Instead of exercise, we choose food. Instead of losing ourselves in worship, we indulge in food. We allow food to become the one that fills all our needs and that is the opposite of healthy self-care.

Let's talk about self-care:

Do you feel guilty when you take time to do what you really need to do? Explain.

How do you feel about taking time to rest? Do you actually do it?

How is your work/life balance? What does that look like in your schedule?

Do you find yourself trying to give to others out of an empty cup? Discuss.

If you were truly taking care of yourself, what would you be doing? Make a list.

Write examples of how you use food instead of healthy self-care.

SELF-CENTEREDNESS

Whoever seeks to preserve his life will lose it, but whoever loses his life will keep it.

LUKE 17:33

When we focus on ourselves, our world contracts as our problems and preoccupations loom large. But when we focus on others, our world expands.

–DANIEL GOLEMAN[14]

———————————

I love the way that quote puts it: Your world only grows smaller if you're at the center of it. Part of healing is realizing that our behaviors affect the other people in our life—even if they appear to only affect us at face value.

Let's talk about self-centeredness:

How have you tried to control or manipulate your family members, friends, co-workers, group members, neighbors, etc.?

How do you react when things do not go your way or when others disagree with you?

In what ways have you been selfish? How has your abuse of food played a part in this?

How has your food abuse and preoccupation with food and your body caused you to be unavailable for important people or events in your life? How is this related to selfishness? Give examples.

SELF-HATRED AND SHAME

There is therefore now no condemnation for those who are in Christ Jesus.
ROMANS 8:1

Shame corrodes the very part of us that believes we are capable of change.
–BRENÉ BROWN[15]

If you had a person in your life treating you the way you treat yourself,
you would have gotten rid of them a long time ago.
–CHERI HUBER[16]

———————

So many of us feel horrible about ourselves from years of compulsive eating, body hate, and extreme diets. But before the eating and the bloated body, we were impacted by our environment. Parents, teachers, or kids from school might have contributed to insulting us in ways that created permanent psychological damage. It may have been teasing from a sibling, sexual abuse by a cousin, being bullied, or often the daily critical voice of a parent who didn't know how to build up a child properly. Whatever the case, the feeling of shame on the inside is a big part of the need to abuse food—and it can quickly morph into a self-perpetuating, toxic cycle of self-abusive behaviors trying to cancel each other out.

Let's talk about self-hatred:

Do you feel self-hatred? How so?

What are the ways you self-perpetuate a cycle of self-hate (thinking, behaviors, relationships, lifestyle)?

How is shame a problem for you? What are the voices of shame in your head?

What is the difference between guilt and shame for you? What do you feel guilty about? What makes you feel shame?

What attitudes, beliefs, or thoughts may hinder you from loving yourself?

What does God say about your being loved and loveable?

Do you think you could ever adopt what the Scripture says about how God loves you?

What would you like to change that would promote self-care as a blood-bought, forgiven child of the living God?

SELF-PITY

Why are you cast down, O my soul, and why are you in turmoil within me?
PSALM 43:5

Suffering isn't ennobling, recovery is.
—CHRISTIAAN N. BARNARD[17]

Feeling sorry for yourself will only lead to depressed moods, and we know that is followed by our insatiable need to numb out those dark feelings with food. They have a saying in Alcoholics Anonymous that reflects this truth: "Poor me, poor me, pour me another drink." We must acknowledge that one step into self-pity can turn into a quick slide into overeating.

Let's talk about self-pity:

When do you notice yourself struggling with self-pity? What are your self-pity themes?

What does it look like and sound like?

When was the last time a spiral into self-pity landed you anywhere good?

Explain your most recent experience of spiraling downward in self-pity and what it did to you.

SEXUAL/ROMANTIC RELATIONSHIPS

"It is not good that the man should be alone; I will make him a helper fit for him."
GENESIS 2:18

Love one another with brotherly affection. Outdo one another in showing honor.
ROMANS 12:10

———————————

It's important to take a thorough look at your intimate relationships. So much of our eating is often a reaction to the ups and downs of relationships. We may eat less when we fall in love and then use food to soothe our aches when we feel hurt, abandoned, or rejected. Or maybe you have found yourself using food to cope because you feel anxious or insecure about your relationships. For some of us, we have abused food so badly during relationship challenges that we ended up creating so much distance and lost connections we desired because of our fear.

You may choose to write a relationship history or timeline highlighting specific characteristics of yourself in relation to each person with whom you've had a relationship.

Let's talk about your relationships:

Make a list of those people, and write about trust, fear, insecurity, promiscuity, cheating, dishonesty, selfishness, molestation, abuse, eating, weight, your self-esteem, and sex in each situation. Were they different? Is there a pattern?

Write about how you dealt with your emotions in these relationships and how it impacted the rest of your life.

YOUR STRENGTHS!

I praise you, for I am fearfully and wonderfully made.
Wonderful are your works; my soul knows it very well.

PSALM 139:14

You are altogether beautiful, my love; there is no flaw in you.

SONG OF SOLOMON 4:7

———————

As we've discussed, Step 4 is often the step that causes people to give up on their recovery. It's difficult, exhausting, and incredibly daunting to make a moral inventory of our character that focuses on how we have fallen short! Furthermore, those of us who struggle in our relationship to food aren't strangers to finding what we don't like about ourselves whether it is in the mirror or emotionally.

But it is just as important in your inventory to take time to articulate your skills or gifts and what you like about yourself! God gave you certain strengths and personally formed you as an individual. The Bible tells us that you are fearfully and wonderfully made! You will need to lean into these strengths to find your way through this recovery.

It's important to take this opportunity in your inventory to list some of the best things about yourself. If you feel that these questions are too hard for you to answer alone, consider asking a close friend or family member to help you with them. You are a uniquely gifted person with many strengths—don't allow fear and shame to make you believe otherwise.

Let's talk about all of your (many) wonderful, God-given strengths:

What do you think you're best at in your job or workplace? If you asked your coworkers the same question about you, how do you think they would answer?

What physical attribute(s) do you most like in yourself? (Be specific—for example, my long fingers, my expressive eyes, my nose that looks like my mother's, my strong legs.)

Think of all the things that your body does for you—for what are you grateful?

What are your strengths in relationships? Are you a good listener, loyal, good at keeping your word, honest? Explain.

What are your strengths in relationships with your spouse, your friends, your siblings, your parents, or your children?

Which of the fruits of the Spirit (see Galatians 5:22-23)—love, joy, peace, patience, kindness, goodness, faithfulness, gentleness, self-control—come easily to you? Which do you practice most regularly in your life?

Ask a few trusted close people in your life the top five strengths they think you have. Write them here when you feel discouraged or weighed down during your process of recovery. Remember, you are not alone! You have support in recovery and in your life.

STEP FOUR
Scripture Meditations

Write out how each verse applies to you. What does it mean to you? How does it relate to your situation?

Jeremiah 17:9-10

The heart is deceitful above all things, and desperately sick; who can understand it? "I the LORD search the heart and test the mind, to give every man according to his ways, according to the fruit of his deeds."

Galatians 6:3-5

For if anyone thinks he is something, when he is nothing, he deceives himself. But let each one test his own work, and then his reason to boast will be in himself alone and not in his neighbor. For each will have to bear his own load.

Colossians 3:5-8

Put to death therefore what is earthly in you; sexual immorality, impurity, passion, evil desire, and covetousness, which is idolatry. On account of these the wrath of God is coming. In these you too once walked, when you were living in them. But now you must put them all away; anger, wrath, malice, slander, and obscene talk from your mouth.

Lamentations 3:40

Let us test and examine our ways and return to the LORD!

Psalm 139:23-24

Search me, O God, and know my heart! Try me and know my thoughts! And see if there be any grievous way in me, and lead me in the way everlasting!

James 1:12

Blessed is the man who remains steadfast under trial, for when he has stood the test he will receive the crown of life, which God has promised to those who love him.

Ephesians 4:31

Let all bitterness and wrath and anger and clamor and slander be put away from you, along with all malice.

STEP
Five

BEING HONEST

STEP FIVE

Being Honest

Admitted to God, to ourselves, and to another human being the exact nature of our wrongs.

Therefore, confess your sins to one another and pray for one another, that you may be healed. The prayer of a righteous person has great power as it is working.

JAMES 5:16

The punishment of every disordered mind is its own disorder.

–ST. AUGUSTINE[18]

OVERVIEW

Step 5 is part of the healing journey that goes beyond looking at our own troubles. We are starting the process of discarding the unhealthy areas that are behind our broken relationship with food. Until you take the step of opening up about the hidden parts of your life, you will remain stuck in your addiction.

Usually the deeper troubles are well-hidden, and no one really knows the truth about our suffering. It takes a lot of stuffing to keep the troubled parts quiet inside. Some of us know we're doing this and are afraid that if we ever stop eating, we might never stop crying from the pain we have been hiding. Others are emotionally unaware because we lost touch with why we were eating so long ago that we don't know what may be there.

In Step 4, we took a thorough look at all the different parts of our story. Now that we're at Step 5, it's time to disclose our story to someone trustworthy. This is the step that will take you out of isolation and free you from the chains of secrecy and silence. It's important to let the right people into our messy selves to help make sense of things. And with the right person listening, we will feel loved and understood.

We will also find that others have similar experiences, which helps us feel less alone, less shame. **It's absolutely necessary that you do not skip this important step.** It is a key to the freedom you are seeking from dependence on food. It's a step of humility, trusting in God and another human being, and a huge step into your peace with food and your body. Say a prayer. Ask for direction for those with whom you may share your inventory. Another recovering person who's been through this process can often be a big help as they know the ropes and can guide you. You may prefer a therapist or a clergy person. Be sure it is someone who will listen compassionately without judgment. This should not be a counseling session or an advice-giving time. It's a time for you to share your full story—the good, the bad, and the ugly. If your support person shares parts of themselves to help you know you are not alone, this can help.

It's wise to include some time for you to discuss your strengths. I think it is helpful to be able to humbly speak the truths that are the best parts of you. Think about if it would help to start or finish with your strengths section. In either case, the affirmations are helpful and empowering.

When you have completed this step, go to a quiet place for prayer, reflection, and rest. Letting out your secrets and making yourself vulnerable before God and another person is a big deal. Rest, recover, and breathe in the refreshing sense of accomplishment. Ask God to show you if there is anything you missed. You will start to feel relieved. You won't have to hide anymore. You will be ready for the next steps of the healing process!

Notes

Daniel didn't want to share some of the pieces of his fourth step because there were areas he didn't want anyone to know. He was okay telling his sponsor most of what he wrote down, so he decided to go ahead and make an appointment. But Daniel decided it was necessary to use therapy to address the more sensitive parts of his inventory. Daniel was able to benefit from the experience of disclosure and the relief that came from letting out his secrets. He could feel his shame slipping away after sharing experiences and feelings he had hidden for over 30 years.

I needed to redo my fourth and fifth steps a few times early on. My first attempts were fairly superficial. I lacked the self-awareness necessary to be thorough. I think the first attempts were a necessary start. Going deeper came with greater insight and understanding. I was grateful for the people who were willing to help me while I fumbled my way through those early days and even today as I continue my reliance on necessary support.

It may feel awkward to ask someone to take the time to listen to your entire fourth step. If you are in a recovery group, another person who is already in the habit of practicing the steps will often welcome the opportunity to help. No matter what, this is an uncomfortable part of your breakthrough. For so many years food was your friend—when you had any troubles at all, it was your most faithful comfort. It may have appeared to help as you found comfort for all your troubles there, but it's time to begin letting people be there for you to help you now instead of food.

Food was a false friend. Carefully chosen people will now become a part of your new life. This step out of isolation is going to be amazing. It isn't easy to make this shift. We all have reasonable excuses for not wanting to rely on people. But pray and ask for guidance about who should be in your support network and pick someone. This is medicine for your problem, and you absolutely need the love and care of others to recover. No one does this alone. I mean no one!

RECOVERY QUESTIONS

1. Now that you have completed your fourth step inventory, how do you feel about sharing your story with another person? Are you ready to disclose your history, defects, crazy thoughts and feelings to God and to another human being?

   _____

   _____

   _____

2. Are you ready to be completely honest and hold nothing back? How will you accomplish this?

   _____

   _____

   _____

3. Is there anything in your inventory you are finding difficult to share? Why?

   _____

   _____

   _____

4. Which of your character defects creates feelings of shame or embarrassment? Describe.

   _____

   _____

   _____

5. What are your hopes surrounding completing Step 5?

   _____

   _____

   _____

6. What are your fears about this level of self-disclosure?

_____

_____

_____

7. Do you have any ideas with whom you might share your inventory?

_____

_____

_____

8. What are the qualities of the person with whom you might choose to share your fifth step?

_____

_____

_____

YOUR STEP FIVE CHALLENGE

After sharing your inventory, write your reaction: What was it like to share your story? What did you learn about being totally open and honest?

What new discoveries did you make about yourself?

How did it feel to share your positive traits?

STEP FIVE
Scripture Meditations

Write out how each verse applies to you. What does it mean to you? How does it relate to your situation?

Proverbs 28:13

Whoever conceals his transgressions will not prosper, but he who confesses and forsakes them will obtain mercy.

James 5:16

Therefore, confess your sins to one another and pray for one another, that you may be healed. The prayer of a righteous person has great power as it is working.

1 John 1:9

If we confess our sins, he is faithful and just to forgive us our sins and to cleanse us from all unrighteousness.

Proverbs 15:22

Without counsel plans fail, but with many advisers they succeed.

Proverbs 20:5

The purpose in a man's heart is like deep water, but a man of understanding will draw it out.

Proverbs 11:14

Where there is no guidance, a people falls, but in an abundance of counselors there is safety.

Proverbs 12:18

There is one whose rash words are like sword thrusts, but the tongue of the wise brings healing.

Galatians 6:2

Bear one another's burdens, and so fulfill the law of Christ.

Galatians 6:1

Brothers, if anyone is caught in any transgression, you who are spiritual should restore him in a spirit of gentleness. Keep watch on yourself, lest you too be tempted.

Proverbs 19:20

Listen to advice and accept instruction, that you may gain wisdom in the future.

STEP

Six

WILLING TO CHANGE

STEP SIX

Willing to Change

Were entirely ready to have God remove all these defects of character.

Humble yourselves before the Lord, and he will exalt you.
JAMES 4:10

OVERVIEW

We have admitted we need real help with our food; more than just a diet, we need a divine intervention. We understand that we need God and other people to help us. We have now begun the "house-cleaning process." And now we are going to invite God into all the areas we identified in our inventories. We need to understand that this step is about gut-level honesty and willingness to change.

For just as we know we're unable to quit overeating without the help of the Lord, the mess inside us that led us to addiction also requires God's help. Many of our twisted ways of behaving and thinking are survival skills. We may even enjoy some of our attitudes and dysfunctional relational behaviors. Who among us hasn't experienced the second-hand benefits of avoidance, which is often based in fear? It has seemed easier not to face our problems than to deal with potentially making mistakes or failure. Some of our character deficits have been adaptive and have, in a sense, "gotten us through." For example, I was a big-time people-pleaser. That might not seem so bad, but when I looked deeper, I realized behind my people-pleasing was deep insecurity and fear of rejection, and I was not true to myself. On the outside, people-pleasing looks "sweet and friendly," but the price tag was the loss of myself, which was a big contributing factor to my addictive eating. Whether we feel empowered when we nurse a good grudge or feel a sense of strength from manipulating others through anger, we must now be willing to lay these down before God and to be changed and healed.

> It is here we are beginning a path of transformation where we become ready to let God have our old selves and be making our way toward becoming more like Him and who He created us to be.

If you don't go forward in your step work, you will go backward. If you want to be free, your healing is dependent on making the necessary changes in the attitudes, behaviors, and beliefs that are part of your self-destruction. At this point, all those defects you identified in Step 4 and shared in Step 5 need to be considered honestly before God. Yes, the fear, anger, resentment, laziness, procrastination, greed, lust, dishonesty, and insecurity all now need to be prayerfully considered. Ask yourself if you are ready and willing to have Him remove these character defects. Be honest about the problems you want to hold on to. It will be impossible to do this completely all at once—and that's okay! Begin by focusing on one or two major areas that need improvement. The point is to be willing to start the process of growing in those areas where we know we need the power of God to help us change. No one gets Step 6 perfectly. It is here we are beginning a path of transformation where we become ready to let God have our old selves and be making our way toward becoming more like Him and who He created us to be. Step 6 is a step we keep taking as we go. We are going to stumble, but if we are willing, we will keep getting better and better.

Notes

Cindy felt like she was more than ready for God to have all of her. She had been close to the Lord since she was young, but this food problem was a source of real guilt and shame. She had readily taken the steps up to this point, and when she arrived at Step 6, she assumed it would be simple: "Of course I want Jesus to take away all of my defects!" But when we looked a little more honestly at her problems, she realized she'd been holding onto some behaviors and attitudes quite strongly. With genuine consideration, she realized she might not be as ready for change as she would like! Cindy noticed how she held grudges, was critical of herself and others, and used food for comfort to the point she admitted she wasn't even sure she could live without that soothing feeling she got from a good binge. On the surface, it seemed this step was simple, but it actually required that Cindy look at herself and her readiness to change more seriously and with gut-level honesty.

My early experiences with Step 6 were quite powerful. For the first time in my life, instead of looking at myself in shame and guilt, I could begin to consider there was hope that maybe I could change and God would do something new with my broken, messy self. It was an entirely new way of thinking about my problems.

In Step 6 you are being asked to become entirely ready to have God remove your defects—which is a very big deal. And it is not so easy to understand (let alone do). The spiritual life is not simple. It isn't necessarily tangible. It isn't practical. It requires a deep understanding and belief in an unseen Power. It requires a leap of faith!

It's easy to pick up a devotional, say some prayers, read a chapter or two from Scripture, attend worship services… but to put your life in God's hands and surrender? That's something to contemplate, because it doesn't make sense to the finite mind. So, I urge you to take time with these steps. Please don't simply go through the motions so you can say you finished them. What's the point of that? Pray and meditate on the verses and concepts here. Think through the questions, and ask the Lord to help you deepen your ability to let Him have _all_ of you.

Are you actually ready to change? Can you imagine being without your flaws? Are you really ready to turn to God and do business?

RECOVERY QUESTIONS

1. What is holding you back? Be specific. In what areas are you feeling less ready?

   _____

   _____

   _____

2. Discuss the parts of your defects you still enjoy. (For example: a little dishonesty in your finances keeps you having a little more; or flirtatiousness may be manipulative, but it gets you what you want; or fear keeps you from failure, but it also keeps you from looking stupid.)

   _____

   _____

   _____

3. Do you believe God can remove your defects? Do you think you can change?

   _____

   _____

   _____

4. How have you changed already?

   _____

   _____

   _____

5. What defects would you rather not change?

   _____

   _____

   _____

6. What do your defects do for you? In other words, what is the benefit of holding on to your behaviors and attitudes?

_____

_____

_____

7. What is the downside of keeping these behaviors and attitudes around?

_____

_____

_____

YOUR STEP SIX CHALLENGE

Write a list of character defects or flaws on one side of a page from your inventory. On the other side, write what you imagine you would be like if you had each defect removed. What would be different? As this is a step of readiness to be changed, it's good to see what you're moving toward. Ask the Lord to show you a new picture of what you might look like without each defect on the list. Be open. Listen. Write what you imagine.

STEP SIX

Scripture Meditations

Write out how each verse applies to you. What does it mean to you? How does it relate to your situation?

Matthew 3:3

For this is he who was spoken of by the prophet Isaiah when he said, "The voice of one crying in the wilderness: 'Prepare the way of the Lord; make his paths straight.'"

Galatians 5:1

For freedom Christ has set us free; stand firm therefore, and do not submit again to a yoke of slavery.

Romans 6:8-14

Now if we have died with Christ, we believe that we will also live with him. We know that Christ, being raised from the dead, will never die again; death no longer has dominion over him. For the death he died he died to sin, once for all, but the life he lives he lives to God. . . . Let not sin therefore reign in your mortal body, to make you obey its passions. Do not present your members to sin as instruments for unrighteousness, but present yourselves to God as those who have been brought from death to life, and your members to God as instruments for righteousness. For sin will have no dominion over you, since you are not under law but under grace.

Ephesians 4:22-24

To put off your old self, which belongs to your former manner of life and is corrupt through deceitful desires, and to be renewed in the spirit of your minds, and to put on the new self, created after the likeness of God in true righteousness and holiness.

Colossians 3:5-13

Put to death therefore what is earthly in you: sexual immorality, impurity, passion, evil desire, and covetousness, which is idolatry. On account of these the wrath of God is coming. In these you too once walked, when you were living in them. But now you must put them all away: anger, wrath, malice, slander, and obscene talk from your mouth. Do not lie to one another, seeing that you have put off the old self with its practices and have put on the new self, which is being renewed in knowledge after the image of its creator. . . . Put on then, as God's chosen ones, holy and beloved, compassionate hearts, kindness, humility, meekness, and patience, bearing with one another and, if one has a complaint against another, forgiving each other; as the Lord has forgiven you, so you also must forgive.

Psalm 119:10-12

With my whole heart I seek you; let me not wander from your commandments! I have stored up your word in my heart, that I might not sin against you. Blessed are you, O LORD; teach me your statutes!

Philippians 3:12-14

Not that I have already obtained this or am already perfect, but I press on to make it my own, because Christ Jesus has made me his own. Brothers, I do not consider that I have made it my own. But one thing I do: forgetting what lies behind and straining forward to what lies ahead, I press on toward the goal for the prize of the upward call of God in Christ Jesus.

STEP

Seven

ACCEPTING GOD'S HELP

STEP SEVEN

Accepting God's Help

> **Humbly asked God to remove our shortcomings.**

If we confess our sins, he is faithful and just to forgive us our sins
and to cleanse us from all unrighteousness.

1 JOHN 1:9

A STEP 7 PRAYER

My Creator, I am willing that You should have all of me, good and bad. I pray that You now remove
from me every single defect of character that stands in the way of my usefulness to You and my fellows.
Grant me strength as I go out from here to do Your bidding.

OVERVIEW

Step 7 is about learning humility. It requires acknowledging the areas of your character, behaviors, attitudes, and beliefs that need to change. In this step, we will put ourselves in a place with God where we open ourselves up to be His and start to see His purpose for our life! Our addiction has gotten in the way of being the version of ourselves that God intended us to be. When we become open and willing to God's removing the blocks and barriers that keep us from truly serving Him and living our best lives, we need to be humble.

Our way is what got us into trouble. We avoided pain with food. Instead of growing along spiritual lines, we hid in terror or tried to make our own way. Though we will never become perfect, we can learn new principles for living. Instead of continuing in our flaws, we now take them to God in a spirit of humility, tell Him all about it, and ask Him to change us. We now ask Him to make us the way He wants us to be. We can be honest about our difficulty letting go of any particular defect—be honest with your Creator. He knows anyway, and your ability to let go will come more easily when you are honest with yourself and with Him.

> Instead of continuing in our flaws, we now take them to God in a spirit of humility, tell Him all about it, and ask Him to change us.

In Step 7, you make a practice of taking your flaws and defects of character in an honest and humble way to the Lord. Without shame and without self-abuse. All our sins have been cleansed on the cross; that work has long been finished. We can go to the Lord in faith that the work of the cross has given us a path to grace where we will be met without blame or shame by our loving Creator who wants us to be free and relieve us of our troubles!

Now, get the idea that He is mad at you out of your head! That is an enormous lie. God sent His Son to die for all of our sins, so when you pray, talk to Him as a child who knows already that you are forgiven. You need Him to help you. You have been working independently of Him in many areas, and this new practice puts you into a place of cooperation and reliance on His power to change, not only your relationship with food and your body, but every other part of your character and life. With humility and God's power, weaknesses can be turned into strengths. We need to learn the true meaning of "more of Him and less of us" (see John 3:30).

Notes

Matt had a history of relapse. One of the challenges he faced was that once he'd begun doing well with his eating, he'd become smug and overconfident. It seemed he needed to fall on his face more than most to learn to practice humility. Troubles in life would pile up, yet Matt never asked anyone for help. He continued to hide negative feelings, avoid conflict, and would not let people know when he was hurting. Matt needed to practice humility in remembering his need for God to keep him sober with food, but he also needed to practice that same humility in all the other areas of life. His own strength was his biggest problem. Matt desperately needed to learn to let people help him and to live out the Scripture: "I can do all things through Him who strengthens me" (see Philippians 4:13).

It's healthy to come to a place of accepting your true self—the good and the bad—and to be okay with being flawed. Frankly, it's helpful to quit seeing yourself as above it all. When you come to grips with knowing that God loves you no matter what, flaws and all, and that He wants you to come as you are, it's life changing.

Recognizing I continually need God's help in every area of my life makes all the difference. I know every day my ability to fully function and thrive depends on my remaining clear that I am in need of the Lord all day in all things. If I want to stay away from food abuse, I need to remain in a place of humility. I can never think I have it all together now. That would be the beginning of the end.

Remember, it's never the shame—it's grace that gets us motivated to change. I hope you will learn to accept the grace of God and His unconditional love for you, and that you will find that you can humbly and without shame take it all to His throne of grace.

RECOVERY QUESTIONS

1. How do you understand "humility"?

_____

_____

_____

2. How does applying humility work when it comes to overcoming overeating?

_____

_____

_____

3. What are your blocks to humility (for example: pride, ego, self-centeredness, intellect)?

_____

_____

_____

4. Explain the differences (using examples) between trying to fix your flaws in your own strength and surrendering to God in letting Him transform you.

_____

_____

_____

5. Are you afraid to ask God for help because of shame and guilt?

_____

_____

_____

6. Do you think you can fix your troubles on your own? How has that worked out so far?

_____

_____

_____

7. How do perfectionistic expectations hold you back from even trying to change or approaching the Lord for help? Do you fear never being able to reach your goals?

_____

_____

_____

8. Accepting and loving ourselves, the good and the bad, is part of the process. Are you able to accept your flaws, or are you self-rejecting? Do you think you can accept and love yourself flaws and all?

_____

_____

_____

9. What are some of the positive sides of your shortcomings? How can you use them for good?

_____

_____

_____

10. What can you do as a daily practice to help remain humble and aware of God's grace and power to change?

_____

_____

_____

YOUR STEP SEVEN CHALLENGE

Take the list you have written and ask one-by-one for God to remove each character defect. Notice if you are aware that you are not ready to let go of any area, and ask for help.

Pray the Step 7 Prayer out loud and reflect (refer to page 110).

Negative Thinking Exercise

Write down some of your most repetitive negative thoughts or lies. Go to three to five trusted friends or family members and ask for feedback about these thoughts, along with some Scripture verses that you can repeat to shut down the lies.

Bad Body Image Exercise

Write a letter to the part of your body you are most unhappy about. Make it a dialogue in which the body part talks back to you and expresses how it feels about the awful way you are talking to yourself. As you continue your dialogue, move toward finally making sincere amends for the awful way you have treated your body.

STEP SEVEN
Scripture Meditations

Write out how each verse applies to you. What does it mean to you? How does it relate to your situation?

Matthew 18:4

Whoever humbles himself like this child is the greatest in the kingdom of heaven.

Psalm 25:9

He leads the humble in what is right, and teaches the humble his way.

Psalm 51:1-2

Have mercy on me, O God, according to your steadfast love; according to your abundant mercy blot out my transgressions. Wash me thoroughly from my iniquity, and cleanse me from my sin!

Luke 14:11

For everyone who exalts himself will be humbled, and he who humbles himself will be exalted.

Proverbs 11:2

When pride comes, then comes disgrace, but with the humble is wisdom.

Romans 3:23-24

For all have sinned and fall short of the glory of God, and are justified by his grace as a gift, through the redemption that is in Christ Jesus.

1 Peter 5:6-10

Humble yourselves, therefore, under the mighty hand of God so that at the proper time he may exalt you, casting all your anxieties on him, because he cares for you. Be sober-minded; be watchful. Your adversary the devil prowls around like a roaring lion, seeking someone to devour. Resist him, firm in your faith, knowing that the same kinds of suffering are being experienced by your brotherhood throughout the world. And after you have suffered a little while, the God of all grace, who has called you to his eternal glory in Christ, will himself restore, confirm, strengthen, and establish you.

1 John 5:14-15

And this is the confidence that we have toward him, that if we ask anything according to his will he hears us. And if we know that he hears us in whatever we ask, we know that we have the requests that we have asked of him.

Jeremiah 18:6

Like the clay in the potter's hand, so are you in my hand.

STEP

Eight

LISTING HARMS

STEP EIGHT

Listing Harms

> **Made a list of all persons we had harmed and became willing to make amends to them all.**

And as you wish that others would do to you, do so to them.
LUKE 6:31

If possible, so far as it depends on you, live peaceably with all.
ROMANS 12:18

OVERVIEW

Now that we have taken a good look at our character flaws and our resentments and fears, we have naturally examined our relationships. Step 8 requires work that makes some people want to run in the opposite direction. We have been burying ourselves in food and running away from our problems, so it makes sense that any preparation to directly deal with the people in our lives would make us want to quit. But we are getting into the real trouble behind our eating addictions, and we need to keep going! Don't forget: God is with you. Don't quit now—you've come so far!

You will make a list of people you have harmed and prepare yourself for amends in this step. It's important to recognize that you may experience feelings of defensiveness. That is natural. It's necessary to face the hurts you have experienced by some of the people on your list. You may have been abused, bullied, or rejected in serious ways, and the wounds can be deep. You may not want to unearth some of these old situations. If you are holding resentments and need to forgive anyone, you must become ready to do so. Our aim is to do the work we need to do to have peace with everyone as much as possible. Remember that holding on to resentment harms you more than the person you resent!

As you compile this list, remember, we are looking at "our own side of the street," even when the others may largely be responsible for problems in the relationship. This process is about us. It is about you. How have you been angry and held grudges? How has your eating caused you to procrastinate or disengage from household chores or activities? How have you controlled others or manipulated them? Have you acted so depressed and shut down that you pushed people away or made them uncomfortable? Have you isolated because of your shame and thus avoided people who love you or disengaged from family? Has your family or work suffered from your avoidance or moodiness? Have you held back feelings and drifted away for fear of speaking up? Have you acted careless or selfish or reckless? Have you been dishonest? Have you stolen and hidden in secret and then lived in guilt for things you did?

> Our aim is to do the work we need to do to have peace with everyone as much as possible.

Make your list, and when you're ready, review it with a trusted person in recovery who can help you sort out the next step. Forgiving yourself is also part of this, so make sure you are on the list. How have you harmed yourself and for what do you need to make amends to yourself? This is really important—guilt for all the mess is rocket fuel for food abuse. We must forgive ourselves!

Notes

At first Jane didn't see that she really had any amends to make—she was a nice person, a loving mom and wife. She didn't realize how her food addiction had really hurt anyone but herself until she dug a little deeper. The more honest she became, the more she realized she needed to make amends for not participating in family life and activities because of her weight. She also withdrew from intimacy in her marriage and had not paid any attention to this problem. Moodiness, avoidance, tiredness—all symptoms of food addiction—were just a few things Jane needed to reconcile. Although Jane was a wonderful woman, she was not exempt from needing to make amends.

I had difficulty making an amends list because I felt like a lot of my troubles were caused by others. I could easily see what they did wrong, but I couldn't see my part. This step helped me learn how to be honest about my behavior and attitudes and to quit focusing on what others were doing to contribute to the problems. It changes everything to look at your own side of the street.

Getting ready to make amends can be terrifying. It will take courage, so stay close to the Lord, and lean into His strength. Facing the people and situations you have avoided for so long is not easy, but this step will propel you closer to freedom. The hard work is worth it. Make sure you have the right support.

As you begin this process, you will find that there are people on your list with whom you are not able to make amends (because it would cause harm), or maybe there's a person on your list who has passed away. It's still a good experience to write about those people, just to ask God to free your heart from unresolved feelings. Don't rush ahead. You will want to prayerfully consider each situation with your support person before moving ahead.

RECOVERY QUESTIONS

1. Is there anything causing you to hold back from making amends? Resentment? Fear? Explain.

_____

_____

_____

2. When you look at your relationships, what are the common themes of your relational patterns? How does your relational pattern cause harm in your relationships?

_____

_____

_____

3. What have you identified in your inventory as causing harm to others?

_____

_____

_____

4. How have you harmed yourself?

_____

_____

_____

5. When you consider the verse, "If possible, so far as it depends on you, live peaceably with all" (Romans 12:18), what does that mean to you?

_____

_____

_____

6. What comes to mind when you consider this verse in your life regarding any particular person or situation?

_____

_____

_____

7. Is there anyone with whom you are not ready or able to make amends? Explain.

_____

_____

_____

8. Who do you need to forgive for harms done to you? For what? Are you ready to forgive? If not, describe the situation.

_____

_____

_____

9. Are there people on your list who may be a potential threat to your safety, or who you have some other serious concern about approaching?

_____

_____

_____

10. Do you need to make financial amends? Are there reasons why that might not be possible, or why by doing so you may cause harm to yourself or someone else? Be honest—how do you feel about making financial amends?

_____

_____

_____

YOUR STEP EIGHT CHALLENGE

Write a list here of all the people you have harmed and how you have harmed them. Focus on your side. Put a check mark next to the names of those people with whom you are not sure you need to make amends.

Are you willing to make amends to the people on your list?

Are you ready to take the next step even if you don't feel like doing it?

Alcoholics Anonymous suggests if you have resentment you aren't ready to forgive, you should pray for that person daily for everything you would pray for yourself. Are you willing to start there, even if you don't mean it? (Remember: This is to relieve *you* of *your* resentment).

STEP EIGHT
Scripture Meditations

Write out how each verse applies to you. What does it mean to you? How does it relate to your situation?

Proverbs 16:6-7

By steadfast love and faithfulness iniquity is atoned for, and by the fear of the LORD one turns away from evil. When a man's ways please the LORD, he makes even his enemies to be at peace with him.

Romans 12:18

If possible, so far as it depends on you, live peaceably with all.

Galatians 6:9-10

And let us not grow weary of doing good, for in due season we will reap, if we do not give up. So then, as we have opportunity, let us do good to everyone, and especially to those who are of the household of faith.

2 Corinthians 2:7-8

So you should rather turn to forgive and comfort him, or he may be overwhelmed by excessive sorrow. So I beg you to reaffirm your love for him.

Luke 6:31

And as you wish that others would do to you, do so to them.

Luke 19:8-10

And Zacchaeus stood and said to the Lord, "Behold, Lord, the half of my goods I give to the poor. And if I have defrauded anyone of anything, I restore it fourfold." And Jesus said to him, "Today salvation has come to this house, since he also is a son of Abraham. For the Son of Man came to seek and to save the lost."

Ecclesiastes 4:9-10

Two are better than one . . . woe to him who is alone when he falls and has not another to lift him up!

MAKING AMENDS

STEP NINE

Making Amends

Made direct amends to such people wherever possible,
except when to do so would injure them or others.

*So if you are offering your gift at the altar and there remember that your brother
has something against you, leave your gift there before the altar and go.
First be reconciled to your brother, and then come and offer your gift.*
MATTHEW 5:23-24

OVERVIEW

When you began recovery, you already started making amends. Changes are already happening in your life, and you are setting things right as you've become more honest, aware, and clear-headed now that you aren't abusing food. In the *AA Big Book*, a long list of promises follows this step, the hope being that once we make our amends, we will experience freedom—no longer fight with cravings—and if we stay in fit spiritual condition, hope to live in peace with food and the past. It even promises you will recoil from temptation as from a hot flame—what a promise!

Some of the amends will come easily, and you will be ready as soon as possible. Some amends may be only partially attainable, and some may do more harm than good. You will also have situations in which direct amends may not be possible (such as death or a closed business). Make sure to go over your list carefully with a sponsor or counselor, and sort through it to determine if there are some amends you need to skip because of potential harm. Also, be sure you are in good condition *emotionally*, so you don't end up giving yourself a reason to abuse food over anxiety or deep-seated hurt. Make sure you are praying and in the right place spiritually as you approach each person on your list. If you aren't ready to manage certain amends, make sure to get the help you need so you don't remain in avoidance—but you don't go ahead before you're ready! Give yourself time, get help as you need it, and don't give up.

It is important to understand that making amends doesn't always mean you are going to re-enter a relationship. You may take responsibility for wrongdoing and make peace with a person, but that does not necessarily mean you will always reconcile. (Forgiveness and peace don't always equal reconciliation.) Sometimes it's best to not be close to someone because they aren't good for you. They could be hurtful or toxic. You still need your heart to be free from resentment and anger, but that doesn't necessarily mean you need to be in a relationship. You can be kind and courteous following amends without inviting the person to your home.

> It is important to understand that making amends doesn't always mean you are going to re-enter a relationship.

Amends can also be related to lifestyle—a change in the way you behave and relate. It's beyond apologies and more a regular action that shows you mean it. Doing things to correct wrongs is amends; it's still good to sit down with people and admit to wrong attitudes and behaviors, acknowledging your willingness to do all that you can to set things right.

Notes

Carla began her recovery process by picking up the 12 Steps and reading them. When she saw the amends step, she said she was never going to take it because there were people she would never forgive in her life. Once we discussed why it was necessary to forgive and how unforgiveness would keep her sick and hinder her recovery, she became more open. We needed to break down how amends would work so it didn't feel awful. There's a good reason we don't start with amends in Step 1. Carla needed help approaching a complicated family member. She had a lot of hurt feelings that needed working through before she could even consider a face-to-face encounter of any sort. She started with praying daily and talking with me about the best way to approach it. Once the time came to address the unresolved issues in the relationship, she was ready. And it went far better than she could ever have expected!

I found amends to be easier than I expected. It was awkward to face people and make necessary changes in complicated relationships and situations. But once I became willing to take this step and make amends, it all came together. I also learned not to do things that required making future amends since this is an ongoing practice. The 12-Step life is a life of honesty, and every day I know I need to do my best to keep things right with people.

I've seen people read the 12 Steps and decide just based on reading Steps 8 and 9 alone that they were not interested! Instead they ran back into the world of fighting with food, trying to diet and never getting control… which is unfortunate, because this process works; it makes sense. There's even research that resentment is behind many illnesses, including cancer, and that people heal when they forgive.[19] It isn't easy, but our body knows. It can actually break down when we carry unresolved relational wounds, guilt, and shame. The unrest inside needs to be quieted for a multitude of reasons. Remember, even when the others don't deserve it, you deserve it! You forgive for yourself—for your peace and freedom! We need to trust God that if we are determined to make peace, we will be in position to fully recover. This is real, breakthrough, life-changing stuff.

RECOVERY QUESTIONS

1. How is making amends the beginning of a continuous process of living in recovery in all areas?

_____

_____

_____

2. How is making amends a part of your surrender to God and His will for your life?

_____

_____

_____

3. What are you most afraid about regarding the amends process—rejection? Defensiveness? Retaliation?

_____

_____

_____

4. Are you able to trust God regarding financial restitution even if you don't know how to work out the situation (practically speaking)?

_____

_____

_____

5. With which amends do you most need help? What are your concerns? Who can help you sort out these concerns?

_____

_____

6. Are there situations wherein it would cause harm to make amends? Explain.

_____

_____

_____

7. What are you doing to make amends to yourself? Be specific based on the list of all the ways you have harmed yourself. What do you need?

_____

_____

_____

8. How are you changing as a "living amends"? Have you already begun, and how is that going? If not, what do you still need to amend in your behaviors and attitudes? Describe.

_____

_____

_____

9. To whom do you need to make direct amends? What is your plan?

_____

_____

_____

10. Are there any amends you are trying to avoid and make excuses about to dodge? If so, why?

_____

_____

_____

YOUR STEP NINE CHALLENGE

When you have completed your amends, write about your overall experience. What did you learn from this process? How was this helpful? How do you feel about your recovery now that you have completed this courageous step?

(Congratulations, by the way, YOU DID IT! You are now officially entering the maintenance steps.)

STEP NINE
Scripture Meditations

Write out how each verse applies to you. What does it mean to you? How does it relate to your situation?

Matthew 5:9

Blessed are the peacemakers, for they shall be called sons of God.

Matthew 5:23-24

So if you are offering your gift at the altar and there remember that your brother has something against you, leave your gift there before the altar and go. First be reconciled to your brother, and then come and offer your gift.

Ephesians 4:32

Be kind to one another, tenderhearted, forgiving one another, as God in Christ forgave you.

Matthew 6:14-15

For if you forgive others their trespasses, your heavenly Father will also forgive you, but if you do not forgive others their trespasses, neither will your Father forgive your trespasses.

Matthew 18:21-22

Then Peter came up and said to him, "Lord, how often will my brother sin against me, and I forgive him? As many as seven times?" Jesus said to him, "I do not say to you seven times, but seventy-seven times."

Colossians 3:12-13

Put on then, as God's chosen ones, holy and beloved, compassionate hearts, kindness, humility, meekness, and patience, bearing with one another and, if one has a complaint against another, forgiving each other; as the Lord has forgiven you, so you also must forgive.

1 Peter 4:8

Above all, keep loving one another earnestly, since love covers a multitude of sins.

Proverbs 10:12

Hatred stirs up strife, but love covers all offenses.

1 Corinthians 13:4-7

Love is patient and kind; love does not envy or boast; it is not arrogant or rude. It does not insist on its own way; it is not irritable or resentful; it does not rejoice at wrongdoing, but rejoices with the truth. Love bears all things, believes all things, hopes all things, endures all things.

STEP

Ten

DAILY HOUSE CLEANING

— STEP TEN —

Daily House Cleaning

Continued to take personal inventory and when we were wrong promptly admitted it.

Therefore let anyone who thinks that he stands take heed lest he fall.

1 Corinthians 10:12

OVERVIEW

Way back in Step 4, we began a major house-cleaning process in our lives. This step is all about learning the practice that keeps your house clean. It's critically important for recovery maintenance to keep problems from building up. We are setting ourselves up for relapse if we let anger and resentment build or if we ignore deep sadness or grief by staying busy, or cover up guilt, or pretend to be okay. To protect yourself from this dilemma, you need to learn to take Step 10 on a daily basis.

There are different ways to take a daily inventory, so you should try out a few to see what fits best. You may even want to use different inventories for different matters. For example, you may use a spot check inventory where you carry a list of character issues and look at it throughout the day. Set reminders to check a few times a day how you are doing in each area. There are checklists online that help you to identify whether something is off so you can work on praying and correcting as you go. If you need help, seek it as soon as possible. The longer you wait, the more vulnerable you are to food abuse, so take care of your attitudes, feelings, and issues as you go as much as possible.

Keeping a feelings list may also help you identify and express the emotions you may not readily understand. Sometimes the only feeling you may experience is "I feel hungry." It's important to learn to understand that if you are following a healthy sustainable food plan, you are probably not hungry for food unless it's mealtime. Thinking about food or thinking you want to eat could be a clue something is "off" inside. Learn to take the cue, pause, and ask what you are feeling. You can write it down, call someone—but don't just eat something, lest you lose the chance to grow emotionally and put yourself back on the slippery slope of addictive eating and cravings.

> **Thinking about food or thinking you want to eat could be a clue something is "off" inside.**

Journaling at a set time each day is another way to take inventory. Writing is extremely helpful in getting to the bottom of your internal mess and making you self-aware and honest about your attitudes, behaviors, feelings, and relationships. You don't have to write long if you do this daily. I find it can be helpful to journal as if you are writing a letter to God. After you complete the journal, try waiting quietly afterward for direction from Him regarding any concerns that have come up that day. If there are any difficulties with which you find you need help, ask a trusted support person. Don't ever let troubles pile up.

Every once in a while, a more thorough house cleaning may be in order. If you do Step 10 and stay on top of your issues, you should be okay, but many of us have heavy burdens and challenges that can create the need for us to go over an area more intensely, or even revisit Step 4 again later in recovery. As believers, we know we are always forgiven, but taking a consistent look at ourselves to see what needs straightening out once a year or once a day is a life-giving practice in understanding God's grace.

Notes

Susan was perplexed about her relapse tendencies. She was trying so hard to recover—by following her food plan, going to meetings, making calls, and reading literature. She couldn't understand why she kept falling. One day at a meeting she heard someone share from a journal, and it hit Susan between the eyes—she had not made Step 10 a daily practice! From that day on, Susan kept a journal and began to talk openly about her discoveries and what was behind her desire to eat. Soon after, the relapsing stopped. She simply hadn't understood how much her inner disturbances were fueling her desire to eat. It was a life-changing moment. Now, she could use other tools instead of eating.

I can't stress enough how vital taking time to check in with my inner thoughts and feelings by writing in a journal or talking to a trusted friend has been in my ability to remain in food freedom. It's truly one of the most important tools I have as I am an emotional person and need to process and straighten myself out often.

Emotional eating is not the same as food addiction. Food addiction has a chemical component, and abstaining from the foods themselves will significantly, if not completely, reduce cravings. Besides the physical triggers of foods and food behaviors, emotional triggers are the most powerful challenge for someone trying to have a healthy relationship with food. As we have talked about in earlier steps, the pairing of food as a comfort, relief, or escape from intense negative emotions has likely been there from an early age, so automatic that there's hardly any thought that another option might be a possibility. Interrupting this process is what the steps are all about. So, Step 10, when you do it diligently, can change the old patterns and create new ones. It will work if you do it, but you must take daily action to get results.

RECOVERY QUESTIONS

1. Are you willing to make time to take inventory each day—both spot checking and journaling?

    _____

    _____

    _____

2. What are the hindrances to your taking Step 10? How might you handle these potential hindrances?

    _____

    _____

    _____

3. On whom can you rely for support in processing the issues that surface as you take your daily inventory?

    _____

    _____

    _____

4. Do you have a tendency toward self-shaming? Are you concerned this step may be an aid in keeping you over-analyzing yourself in a negative way?

    _____

    _____

    _____

5. How can you do your inventory so it's helpful and encouraging rather than shaming?

    _____

    _____

    _____

6. Can you put a place in your inventory each day for affirmations? Are you uncomfortable with self-affirmation?

_____

_____

_____

7. What can you do to help yourself grow in learning to see the best parts of yourself each day?

_____

_____

_____

8. Are you willing to make a habit of correcting your mistakes or wrongdoings as quickly as possible?

_____

_____

_____

9. Do you still tend to blame others for your reactions, or have you made a habit of looking at your reactions without blame?

_____

_____

_____

10. Are you ready to be open with yourself and your supports to "clean up your side of the street," regardless of what may be happening on the other side?

_____

_____

_____

YOUR STEP TEN CHALLENGE

Journal

Write your feelings and thoughts daily for this week—go over the day, and write about what went well and what didn't (even the small stuff). Look at patterns of anger, fear, self-pity, jealousy, or procrastination. Notice how often different "defects of character" (see Step Six) arise and how you feel—do you want to eat when they do?

Spot Check Inventory

Carry a piece of paper with a list of character issues to review for self-awareness. Try this a few times a day for one week, correcting attitudes as you go. Use supports to help with course correcting; keep an eye on anger, resentment, fear, anxiety, procrastination, dishonesty, etc.

STEP TEN
Scripture Meditations

Write out how each verse applies to you. What does it mean to you? How does it relate to your situation?

1 Corinthians 10:12

Therefore let anyone who thinks that he stands take heed lest he fall.

Romans 12:2-3

Do not be conformed to this world, but be transformed by the renewal of your mind, that by testing you may discern what is the will of God, what is good and acceptable and perfect. For by the grace given to me I say to everyone among you not to think of himself more highly than he ought to think, but to think with sober judgment, each according to the measure of faith that God has assigned.

Philippians 2:12-13

Therefore, my beloved, as you have always obeyed, so now, not only as in my presence but much more in my absence, work out your own salvation with fear and trembling, for it is God who works in you, both to will and to work for his good pleasure.

Acts 3:19

Repent therefore, and turn back, that your sins may be blotted out.

1 John 1:9

If we confess our sins, he is faithful and just to forgive us our sins and to cleanse us from all unrighteousness.

2 Chronicles 7:14

If my people who are called by my name humble themselves, and pray and seek my face and turn from their wicked ways, then I will hear from heaven and will forgive their sin and will heal their land.

1 Timothy 4:7-8

Have nothing to do with irreverent, silly myths. Rather train yourself for godliness; for while bodily training is of some value, godliness is of value in every way, as it holds promise for the present life and also for the life to come.

Romans 12:19

Beloved, never avenge yourselves, but leave it to the wrath of God, for it is written, "Vengeance is mine, I will repay, says the Lord."

2 Peter 3:9

The Lord is not slow to fulfill his promise as some count slowness, but is patient toward you, not wishing that any should perish, but that all should reach repentance.

STEP

Eleven

CONNECTING WITH GOD

STEP ELEVEN

Connecting with God

> Sought through prayer and meditation to improve our conscious contact with God, as we understood Him, praying only for knowledge of His will for us and the power to carry that out.

Let the Word of Christ dwell in you richly.
COLOSSIANS 3:16

OVERVIEW

In Step 11 the primary focus is on our spirituality. For those of you who are believers, you may already have a regular prayer and meditation practice. If not, or if you feel like your relationship with God needs some renovation, this is the step where you should examine your connection with God and work to strengthen it.

Paul tells us in 1 Thessalonians 5:17 to "pray without ceasing." In Ephesians 5:18, we are commanded to "be filled with the Spirit" instead of being drunk with wine (for which we can substitute sugar, flour, volume, fat, and salt). Drawing near to the Lord is the solution—it's the food we've always needed. Making it your business to feed yourself spiritually as if your life depends on it is essential. Without your spiritual connection, you will go hungry. You will lack power and require something fast and false to fill the void.

The Alcoholics Anonymous 12 Step book offers a simple way of meditating that can be applied to almost any devotional, 12 Step reading, or Scripture. It suggests taking a prayer or reading one line at a time, carefully contemplating each part. This takes your mind off you, your troubles, the world's

150

troubles, and for that moment, you are reading and reflecting only on the passage at hand. This meditation exercise creates an ability to focus. You may use a journal to write insights and reflections as well. This practice is great for those who tend to have wandering minds.

Music, and worship music in particular, can be extremely helpful in creating a spiritual experience. When you are ready for your time with God, sing a song you have memorized or play a recorded worship song to help you draw close to the Lord. Scripture tells us that God inhabits the praises of His people, so a time of praise through song, gratitude lists, or other types of thankfulness can guide you toward a more meaningful spiritual connection.

Another helpful prayer practice for wandering minds is using a prayer journal to write to God in letter form (we talked about this practice in the last step as well). See if the Lord has something to say to you. Maybe a word will be given in your spirit as you learn to listen for His voice. Writing down in faith what you feel He may be saying can also help, but be careful to see that what you are getting lines up with His Word, reflecting His love and grace.

Praying alongside others is also helpful, especially if you are feeling stuck or in need. A brother or sister in the Lord praying with you can be a source of encouragement and could help you get unstuck when you're in trouble.

You may have other practices you have learned through your religious life, or you may still be unsure. That's okay. It's good to explore and remain open to find your right path of spiritual connection. Though a religious group may be part of your spiritual development, this is about your personal relationship with a loving God whom you can talk to and hear from every day.

Notes

Step 11 made all the difference for Joe. He found that starting and ending his day with prayer and meditation helped him feel closer to God. He felt more at peace, aiding him to make better choices with food when life got complicated. He also experienced a deeper sense of fulfillment as he found himself growing through his daily readings and meditations. His times of prayer and reflection provided direction for his days and life.

Like Joe, my connection to God is the food that I need. Spending time in prayer and meditation was difficult at first. I had no patience to sit still and wait or rest or read and pay attention. But I learned to practice these things and to press in until I came to understand this was the Power Source I need every day—the fuel for living fully.

As with the daily inventory in Step 10, it's crucial to make the daily routine of prayer and meditation a commitment. Some people struggle with this step for a variety of understandable reasons: not being able to focus, not being able to connect with God, not really believing, or simply being too busy. Here's the bottom line: This is the best medicine to treat food addiction. If you take it, you will recover. If you don't, you will remain in the battle. It's your choice. The discipline of a prayer and meditation practice is challenging. Ask God to show you the best path. There may be a new way that will work well for you if you are open and willing. Ask people who you know are spiritually strong about their prayer and meditation practices—try their practice on for size. You may find a new connection along the way. Don't quit chasing after your spiritual connection until you hit your groove. And then keep going!

RECOVERY QUESTIONS

1. What has been your prior experience with prayer and meditation?

   _____

   _____

   _____

2. Reflect on your experience with discovering God's will for your life.

   _____

   _____

   _____

3. What are your difficulties or blocks to prayer and meditation?

   _____

   _____

   _____

4. What is your current prayer and meditation practice, and how could you improve on it?

   _____

   _____

   _____

5. In what ways do you know that God is speaking to you?

   _____

   _____

   _____

6. How well do you feel you are doing at living in His will rather than your own?

_____

_____

_____

7. Are you willing to make every effort to make prayer and meditation a daily practice? To seek the Lord prayerfully in all things?

_____

_____

_____

8. What do you need to put in place practically to help you make Step 11 a daily practice?

_____

_____

_____

YOUR STEP ELEVEN CHALLENGE

Step 11 can take the form of any of the following. Try them out and see what works best for you!

- Write out a journal entry about the day—the good, the bad—what needs work and what's a praise. (Remember: Keep track through the day and repair as you go.)

- Make a daily gratitude list.

- Sing or listen to worship songs.

- Meditate on one or more daily readings.

- As you pray: thank God for recovery, ask Him for another day, align yourself with God's will, express concerns for yourself and others honestly and openly. Be real when you pray—God can handle it.

- Spend time reading your Bible and recovery literature.

- Daily meditations can be as simple as writing out how each Bible verse applies to you. What does it mean to you? How does it relate to your situation?

Your challenge is to build a disciplined daily routine that will strengthen your connection to God!

STEP ELEVEN
Scripture Meditations

Write out how each verse applies to you. What does it mean to you? How does it relate to your situation?

Colossians 3:2

Set your mind on things that are above, not on things that are on earth.

Psalm 25:4-5

Make me to know your ways, O LORD; teach me your paths. Lead me in your truth and teach me, for you are the God of my salvation; for you I wait all the day long.

Philippians 4:6-7

Do not be anxious about anything, but in everything by prayer and supplication with thanksgiving let your requests be made known to God. And the peace of God, which surpasses all understanding, will guard your hearts and your minds in Christ Jesus.

Philippians 4:8

Finally, brothers, whatever is true, whatever is honorable, whatever is just, whatever is pure, whatever is lovely, whatever is commendable, if there is any excellence, if there is anything worthy of praise, think about these things.

Isaiah 30:21

And your ears shall hear a word behind you, saying, "This is the way, walk in it," when you turn to the right or when you turn to the left.

John 15:4-5

Abide in me, and I in you. As the branch cannot bear fruit by itself, unless it abides in the vine, neither can you, unless you abide in me. I am the vine; you are the branches. Whoever abides in me and I in him, he it is that bears much fruit, for apart from me you can do nothing.

1 Thessalonians 5:16-18

Rejoice always, pray without ceasing, give thanks in all circumstances; for this is the will of God in Christ Jesus for you.

STEP

Twelve

WALKING THE WALK

STEP TWELVE

Walking the Walk

> Having had a spiritual awakening as a result of these Steps, we tried to carry this message to other overeaters and to practice these principles in all our affairs.

May the God of hope fill you with all joy and peace in believing,
so that by the power of the Holy Spirit you may abound in hope.

ROMANS 15:13

Brothers, if anyone is caught in any transgression, you who are spiritual should restore him in a spirit of gentleness. Keep watch on yourself, lest you too be tempted.

GALATIANS 6:1

OVERVIEW

When we embrace each of the 12 Steps and depend on God to guide us through them, we begin to see something wonderful: progress! A spiritual awakening will also come as a result of practicing these steps while ridding ourselves of our old addictive behaviors. If we are depending on God, surrendering all of our shortcomings, relying on Him for direction, and doing all that we can to live in peace, we see that we are no longer fighting with food, obsessing with numbers on a scale, or living like our old selves!

If we have not experienced this yet, there may be areas we have not surrendered—unresolved issues in our inventories or amends that still need to be made. Do not be discouraged. Sometimes a spiritual awakening happens slowly; you will notice you are changing over time, and some of you may have more dramatic spiritual experiences. No matter your pace, keep seeking daily to practice the 12 Steps and trust the process. It is not the pace that matters; it is only reaching the freedom from addiction you've desired.

Once you have begun to make progress in your recovery journey, it is time to start getting involved with helping others who have similar struggles. Most people find it extremely freeing to meet someone who is willing to tell the truth about their own struggle with food and weight. Since isolation is such a big part of addiction, it is divine to encounter another person who has been in the same mess and knows something about the agony of defeat and how to find freedom. Sharing your recovery story, how you struggled, and what has helped you can be lifesaving to someone in bondage. Always stay ready and willing to offer help when you have a chance to share your experience and strength with someone in need.

It is also important that you are not too eager to push your recovery on people who are not interested. Your zeal may alienate people who don't really want what you have. Be careful not to assume when people ask that they actually want a true recovery process—most people are looking for quick-fix diets.

Practicing these principles in all our affairs indicates that recovery is a lifestyle. When we pray, or when we identify areas in our inventories that need addressing, we need to apply the truth of God's Word. So, if we're angry, we need to straighten out our struggles and make peace. If we have been dishonest, we need to repair any damage and make matters right. Meditating on God's Word gives instruction for living, and we need to practice what we learn so we become more like Him. We are called to imitate Him. Our work is to align our will with His. This is the only way to stay truly healthy and free!

Notes

Charlie discovered that his recovery was working far better once he started to engage in supporting other people. The responsibility to bring hope and strength to his new struggling companions gave him a new reason to take his own recovery more seriously. It had been easier to make bad choices and slip in and out of trouble with food until he realized the wonderful blessing of partnership. Before he was ready to help his new companion, he needed to practice his own recovery consistently. Once he committed to his food plan, a daily practice of prayer, honest self-reflection, and meditation, he was ready to give what he had been given to someone else. This was exactly what recovery is all about—the beauty of people with similar troubles helping each other. And it works! Charlie finally had the courage once he had a little stability in his own life, and the results to this day have been fantastic.

The first time I was asked to help someone, I did not feel at all equipped. I was still such a mess and did not see what I could offer anyone. Nevertheless, opportunities were knocking, and it was time to put aside self-doubt and offer some help. Not only is helping people reinforcing, it also helps me get out of myself and realize I can be of use to others even though I'm a work in progress, which I believe I will always be.

It's powerful to realize the growth potential when a person takes on the challenge of helping someone else. People in recovery circles say it all the time—to be able to stay sober, I need to help someone else. But so many of us feel inadequate to help. We look at ourselves and all the years of difficulty and wonder what we can possibly have to offer another person. **And yet, this is a significant part of our freedom: We need to help other people to stay free ourselves.**

But that's not all Step 12 is about. This step tells us to practice these principles in all our affairs. My friends, this is a lifetime process of continual transformation. Don't worry about perfection; just be willing to keep growing along spiritual lines all the days of your life.

Our recovery is dependent on our being in fit spiritual condition. As you practice this program, it will become second nature to surrender to God, pray, meditate, and deal with issues as they arise. And I promise, it won't always feel as tough as it has going through this workbook. At some point it will be second nature.

RECOVERY QUESTIONS

1. Now that you are on Step 12, write your story. What was it like before, what have you learned, and what has changed? (Be prepared to tell your story... you may save someone's life.)

   _____

   _____

   _____

2. What can you share at this point about what you have learned and how you have changed?

   _____

   _____

   _____

3. How do you feel about sharing with others or helping others? What strengths do you bring and what are your hindrances?

   _____

   _____

   _____

4. Are you willing to help others even if you are not perfect and you are still a work in progress?

   _____

   _____

5. What does it mean to practice these principles in all our affairs? Describe how you are practicing the 12 Steps in your life.

   _____

   _____

   _____

6. What still needs improvement in your recovery practice?

_____

_____

_____

7. Do you see yourself relying more on God and less on yourself? How do you see Him at work in you?

_____

_____

_____

YOUR STEP TWELVE CHALLENGE

Share your story or help someone in need. You may feel like you are still new to recovery, but if you have made it all the way to Step 12, you are definitely ready to offer help to someone new to recovery. Pray, be open, and offer to be involved in helping in some way. If you attend 12-Step meetings, maybe you can tell your story. If there is someone new, maybe you can call and offer to help get them acclimated to recovery. Give it a try!

Remember: Take recovery one day at a time and never give up!

STEP TWELVE
Scripture Meditations

Write out how each verse applies to you. What does it mean to you? How does it relate to your situation?

Luke 6:49

But the one who hears and does not do them is like a man who built a house on the ground without a foundation. When the stream broke against it, immediately it fell, and the ruin of that house was great.

Philippians 4:9

What you have learned and received and heard and seen in me—practice these things, and the God of peace will be with you.

1 Thessalonians 5:14

And we urge you, brothers, admonish the idle, encourage the fainthearted, help the weak, be patient with them all.

1 Corinthians 9:22

To the weak I became weak, that I might win the weak. I have become all things to all people, that by all means I might save some.

Isaiah 40:1

Comfort, comfort my people, says your God.

Hebrews 3:13

But exhort one another every day, as long as it is called "today," that none of you may be hardened by the deceitfulness of sin.

1 Thessalonians 5:11

Therefore encourage one another and build one another up, just as you are doing.

Genesis 2:18

*Then the L*ORD *God said, "It is not good that the man should be alone; I will make him a helper fit for him."*

Philippians 2:4

Let each of you look not only to his own interests, but also to the interests of others.

Hebrews 10:25

Not neglecting to meet together, as is the habit of some, but encouraging one another, and all the more as you see the Day drawing near.

A NEW BEGINNING

———— A NEW BEGINNING ————

Now that you have completed your steps, let this be the start of a lifetime of step studies and reinforcing of what you have learned. This needs to be a maintenance lifestyle if you want to live in freedom. I am so thankful to have been part of your recovery journey. Let me leave you with this special blessing on your newfound freedom:

May you be blessed with freedom from temptation and a lifetime of living sanely with food and your body.

May you find healthy coping strategies for living and tools that will enable you to live victoriously all the days of your life.

May you find your true satisfaction in a deep abiding connection with the God of the universe.

May you be truly Satisfied.

Amen!

"Yesterday, Today, Tomorrow"
–Author Unknown

There are two days in every week
about which we should not worry,
two days which should be kept free of fear and apprehension.
One of these days is YESTERDAY
with its mistakes and cares,
its faults and blunders,
its aches and pains.
YESTERDAY has passed forever beyond our control.
All the money in the world cannot bring back YESTERDAY.
We cannot undo a single act we performed;
we cannot erase a single word we said.
YESTERDAY is gone.
The other day we should not worry about is TOMORROW
with its possible adversities, its burdens,
its large promise and poor performance.
TOMORROW is also beyond our immediate control.
TOMORROW's sun will rise,
either in splendor or behind a mask of clouds—
but it will rise.
Until it does, we have no stake in TOMORROW,
for it is yet unborn.
This leaves only one day—TODAY.
Any man can fight the battles of just one day;
it is only when you and I add the burdens of those two awful eternities—
YESTERDAY and TOMORROW—
that we break down.
It is not the experience of TODAY that drives men mad—
it is remorse or bitterness for something which happened YESTERDAY
and the dread of what TOMORROW may bring.
Let us, therefore, live but ONE day at a time.

——— ACKNOWLEDGMENTS ———

Sincere thanks to the Dexterity team for believing in this work and putting endless effort into providing life-giving tools for people who can benefit from these books. To Matt West, thank you for your commitment to building Dexterity, providing support, friendship, faith, and diligence in every project. Your leadership is awesome, and I will always be grateful to you for understanding the significance of providing life-changing books to the world. Thank you to Kim West for keeping the business going behind the scenes and always being a blessing. Also big thanks to Kathryn Notestine for doing a great job managing many of the aspects of publishing. I am especially grateful to those involved in writing and editing—Matt Litton, you are such a great friend of this work and a blessing to know and work with. I am so grateful to have your help. To Rachel Ryan and Jessie Epstein, thank you both for doing an amazing job. Thank you to Stacey Owens and Lauren Bryan for putting the finishing touches on the manuscript. Also thank you, Marissa Begin, for your help with making sure the world finds out about this resource. You were all great to have on my team.

To my family, especially my precious daughters Danielle, Jessie, Arielle, and Jordan and my dear friends and colleagues (you all know who you are), thank you for being available to support me in so many ways. I would never be able to do anything good without your love and prayers.

Above all I give thanks to God, who gave the message of recovery to a bunch of alcoholics many years ago; by their efforts to pass it on, people with all kinds of troubles, like me, have found help.

NOTES

1. Brené Brown, *Braving the Wilderness: The Quest for True Belonging and the Courage to Stand Alone*. New York: Random House, 2019.

2. Brian Zahnd, *Unconditional? The Call of Jesus to Radical Forgiveness*. Lake Mary, FL: Charisma House, 2011.

3. A.A. World Services, Inc. *Alcoholics Anonymous: Big Book*. 1993.

4. Brené Brown, *Rising Strong*. New York: Random House USA, 2017.

5. Franklin D. Roosevelt, quoted in Jeryl Brunner, "On the Anniversary of FDR's Birth, Read His 15 Greatest Quotes", *Parade*, January 30, 2015, https://parade.com/370879/jerylbrunner/on-the-anniversary-of-fdrs-birth-read-his-15-greatest-quotes/.

6. Dennis Palumbo, "Getting Out of Your Own Way." *Psychology Today*, March 27, 2013, http://www.psychologytoday.com/us/blog/hollywood-the-couch/201303/getting-out-your-own-way.

7. Robert Brault, "Quotes for the Uptown Crowd", *The New Robert Brault Reader* (blog), http://rbrault.blogspot.com/p/quotes.html.

8. Suzy Kassem, "Quotes", Suzy Kassem (website), http://suzykassem.com/.

9. Henry Cloud and John Townsend, *Boundaries: When to Say Yes, When to Say No to Take Control of Your Life*. Grand Rapids, MI: Zondervan, 1992.

10. C. S. Lewis, *Mere Christianity*. New York: Macmillan, 1967.

11. Søren Kierkegaard, *Provocations: Spiritual Writings of Kierkegaard*. Walden, NY: Plough Publishing House, 2014.

12. bell hooks, u.p.

13. Parker J. Palmer, *Let Your Life Speak: Listening for the Voice of Vocation.* San Francisco, CA: Jossey-Bass, 2000.

14. Daniel Goleman, *Social Intelligence: The New Science of Human Relationships.* London: Arrow Books, 2013.

15. Brené Brown, *I Thought It Was Just Me: Women Reclaiming Power and Courage in a Culture of Shame.* New York: Gotham, 2007.

16. Cheri Huber and June Shiver. *There Is Nothing Wrong with You: Regardless of What You Were Taught to Believe; Going Beyond Self-Hate: A Compassionate Process for Learning to Accept Yourself Exactly as You Are.* Murphys, CA: Keep It Simple Books, 2001.

17. Christiaan N. Barnard, quoted in Sheila Ballentyne, "Rancho Libido and Other Hot Spots", *New York Times*, April 28, 1985, https://www.nytimes.com/1985/04/28/books/rancho-libido-and-other-hot-spots.html.

18. St. Augustine, u.p.

19. Loren L. Toussaint, David R. Williams, and Everett L. Worthington, eds. *Forgiveness and Health: Scientific Evidence and Theories Relating Forgiveness to Better Health.* New York: Springer, 2015.

ABOUT THE AUTHOR

Rhona Epstein, Psy.D is a licensed psychologist, addictions counselor, and marriage and family therapist in the Philadelphia area and the author of *Food Triggers: End Your Cravings, Eat Well and Live Better* and *Satisfied: A 90-Day Spiritual Journey Toward Food Freedom*. Her work has been featured in numerous publications, including *Woman's World* and *Christian Counseling Today*. For more than thirty years, she's led seminars, conferences, and therapeutic workshops to help people overcome food addiction and its underlying issues.

Dr. Rhona received her doctorate in clinical psychology from Chestnut Hill College and her master's degree in counseling psychology from Temple University. After earning her master's degree, she received a certificate in marriage and family therapy from the Council for Relationships at the University of Pennsylvania. Fueled by her own experience and recovery from food addiction, she is passionate about addressing the needs of the whole person (mind, body, and spirit). Dr. Rhona lives and practices in the Philadelphia, PA area; *The Satisfied Workbook: A Spiritual Guide to Recovery and Food Freedom* is her third book.